Human Rights
Have No Borders

The editors and publishers acknowledge with gratitude the financial support of ColourBooks, Dublin, who sponsored the printing of this volume.

Published in 1998 by Marino Books
16 Hume Street Dublin 2
Tel: (01) 661 5299; Fax: (01) 661 8583
e.mail: books@marino.ie

Trade enquiries to CMD Distribution
55A Spruce Avenue
Stillorgan Industrial Park
Blackrock County Dublin
Tel: (01) 294 2556; Fax: (01) 294 2564

© Introduction Amnesty International
Rathgar Group, Dublin
© Individual poems the contributors
The Acknowledgements page is an
extension of this copyright notice

ISBN 1 86023 079 2
A CIP record for this title is available
from the British Library

Cover design by Shaughn McGrath
'From the Republic of Conscience'
graphics designed by
D. & M. McCarthy
Printed by ColourBooks
Baldoyle Industrial Estate Dublin 13

Human Rights
Have No Borders

Voices of Irish Poets

Edited by
Kenneth Morgan
and Almut Schlepper

Acknowledgements

Grateful acknowledgement is made to the following poets and publishers for permission to reproduce copyright material.

Leland Bardwell for 'Prison Poem'; Sara Berkeley for 'A Thousand Letters'; Carcanet Press for 'The War Horse' from Collected Poems (1995) by Eavan Boland; Dermot Bolger for 'Lines for an Unknown Uncle' from Taking My Letters Back: New and Selected Poems (1998), published by New Island Books; Pat Boran for 'Flesh' from Or Volge L'Ano: The Year's Turning, published by Dedalus Press; Rory Brennan for 'Ballad of the Yes Man' from The Sea on Fire (1978), published by Dolmen Press; Heather Brett for 'The Man Who Crushed Butterflies'; Paddy Bushe for 'Assemblage'; Louise C. Callaghan for 'Paquida', published in Beyond Bedlam, edited by Ken Smith and Matthew Sweeney (Anvil Poetry Press); Moya Cannon for 'Going for Milk'; Philip Casey for 'An Indian Dreams of the River' from After Thunder (1985), published by Raven Arts Press; Salmon Publishing for 'Deadbeat' from Proximity (forthcoming in 2000) by Patrick Chapman; Sean Clarkin for 'The Dissenting Voice'; Harry Clifton for 'The House of the Deportee'; Gallery Press for 'Though There Are Torturers' from Two for a Woman, Three for a Man (1980) by Michael Coady; Declan Collinge for 'Chorus'; Roz Cowman and Salmon Publishing for 'Peanuts' from The Goose Herd (1989) by Roz Cowman; David Croft for 'Any Name You Could Possibly Think Of'; Anthony Cronin for '1798'; Leo Cullen for 'The View Above Rosenallis'; Dedalus Press for 'Still Life' from Three Songs of Home (1998) by Tony Curtis; Dedalus Press for 'After Chernobyl' from The Voice of the Hare (1997) by Padraig Daly; Gerald Dawe for 'Summer Journal'; Seamus Deane for 'Buying Time'; Celia de Fréine for 'There Was a War On'/ Bhí Cogadh ar Siúl; Greg Delanty for 'The Emerald Isle'; Black Pepper Press for 'Assimilation/ An Dubh Ina Gheal' from Sentences of Earth and Stone (1996) by Louis de Paor; Bloodaxe for 'Changeling' from Entering the Mare (1997) by Katie Donovan; Theo Dorgan for 'It Goes On'; Noel Duffy for 'Homecoming'; Oliver Dunne for 'Death of the Renaissance'; Paul Durcan and Blackstaff Press for 'Amnesty' from Daddy, Daddy (1990); The Goldsmith Press Ltd. for 'Peace' from Elegies by Desmond Egan; Peter Fallon and Gallery Press for 'World Peace' from News of the World (1998); Gabriel Fitzmaurice for 'The Day Christ Came to Moyvane'; Salmon Publishing for 'In the Free World' from Up She Flew (1991) by Michael Gorman; Gallery Press for 'We Change the Map' from A Furious Place (1996) by Kerry Hardie; Michael Hartnett for 'A Prayer for Sleep'; Anne Haverty for 'She Dreamed of a Washing Machine'; Gallery Press for 'My House is Tiny' from What the Hammer (1998) by Dermot Healy; Seamus Heaney for 'From the Republic of Conscience' (1989); Michael D. Higgins for 'Between Seasons'; Fred Johnston for 'The Poet Laments the Uselessness of his Verse'; Fergal Keane for 'Just the Facts'; Anne Le Marquand Hartigan for 'Dear Life'; Michael Longley for 'Ceasefire' and 'All of These People'; Brian Lynch for 'Three Pieces in the Form of a Pair'; Story Line Press, PO Box 1108, Ashland, OR 97520-0052, USA for 'The Peace-Keeper' from The Wind Beyond the Wall (1990) by Joan McBreen; Blackstaff Press for 'Lucy's Song' from The Blue Globe (1998) by Catherine Phil MacCarthy; Steve MacDonogh and Brandon Book Publishing for 'Com an Áir' from By Dingle Bay and Blasket Sound by Steve MacDonogh; Medbh McGuckian for 'Red Trial'; Gallery Press for 'Kinsale' from Selected Poems (1990) by Derek Mahon; Oxford University Press for lines by Osip Mandelstam from 'Voronezh', 1935, translated by Clarence Brown and W. S. Merwin in Osip Mandelstam: Selected Poems 1936-1970 (1973); Paula Meehan for 'Those Nights' from Reading the Sky (1987) published by Dolmen Press; Salmon Publishing for 'The Same Child' from Snowfire (1995) by Noel Monahan; John Montague for 'Death of Maidens'; Paul Muldoon for 'The Drowned Blackbird' and for 'Black'; Richard Murphy for 'Prison'; Eiléan Ní Chuilleanáin for 'Translation'; Nuala Ní Dhomhnaill for 'Dubh'; Salmon Publishing for 'Lament for Babi Yar' from Reading the Sunflowers in September (1990) by Mary O'Donnell; Chatto & Windus for 'The State of the Nation' from The Weakness (1991) by Bernard O'Donoghue; Anvil Press Poetry for '1989' from Long Short Story (1993) by Dennis O'Driscoll; Desmond O'Grady for 'In the House of Commons' from The Road Taken: Poems 1956-1996 (1996) published by University of Salzburg Press; Salmon Publishing for 'Antigone' from The Troubled House by Sheila O'Hagan; Mary O'Malley for 'The Abandoned Child'; Cló Iar-Chonnachta Teo. for 'Do Isaac Rosenberg' by Cathal Ó Searcaigh and for 'For Isaac Rosenberg' by Frankie Sewell from Out in the Open (1997); Bloodaxe Books for extract from 'Etty Hillesum' from Our Double Time (1998) by Micheal O'Siadhail ; Michael O'Sullivan for 'And After This Our Exile'; Faber and Faber for 'Palestinian Free State' from Walking A Line (1994) by Tom Paulin; Justin Quinn for 'Manumission'; Reality Street Editions for 'Steps' from Steps (1998) by Maurice Scully; Peter Sirr for 'The Universal Remote'; Eithne Strong for 'Credo' from Sarah, in Passing (1974), published by Dolmen Press; Collins Press for 'The Fire People' from Mathematics & Other Poems (1996) by William Wall; David Wheatley for 'Lines on the Unknown Soldier'; Dedalus Press for 'Fire and Snow and Carnevale' from Selected Poems (1996) by Macdara Woods.

Thoughts on the 50th Anniversary of the Universal Declaration of Human Rights

Mary Robinson, United Nations High Commissioner for Human Rights and former President of Ireland

When we look at the situation of human rights around the world, it is evident that the 50th anniversary of the Universal Declaration is not an occasion for celebration. Rather it should be a time for reflection and re-dedication to working towards making the principles elaborated in the preamble and thirty articles of the Declaration a reality in the lives of all people, everywhere.

I would ask those commemorating the 50th anniversary to recognise the indivisibility and interdependence of human rights. We cannot make progress on civil and political rights without also addressing entitlements to economic, social and cultural rights and the right to development.

Our theme for this year reflects the broadly based approach which I believe is essential to achieving a more balanced and constructive dialogue on human rights. The theme *all human rights for all* reflects this approach and poses a tough challenge for governments, non-governmental organisations, academics, the media and civil society generally. My work depends on partnerships with government and others around the world and the support of all who believe that the Universal Declaration speaks as clearly and urgently today as it did fifty years ago.

in memoriam Margaret Whooley

Contents

Introduction

You took away all the oceans and all the room
You gave me my shoe-size in earths with bars around it
Where did it get you? Nowhere.
You left me my lips, and they shape words, even in silence.

Osip Mandelstam (1935)

It began in Almut's kitchen one dark December night last year and all of us at our local Amnesty International group agreed it was a great idea. We would publish an anthology of contemporary Irish poetry to commemorate the 50th anniversary of the Universal Declaration of Human Rights. The book would be a celebration of hope and courage: poets, who universally lend expression to the emotions we all share, could act as the voice of those too often brutally silenced.

We began by writing to poets throughout the country and further afield. In the weeks that followed, the kitchen became a virtual reading room, the table piled high with the thoughtful work of contributors to our anthology. But if the response to our request was surprising, even more staggering were the depth and breadth of the poems themselves. From the 1798 Rebellion to the Irish peace process; from the suppression of Chinese dissidents to the plight of aboriginals in Australia; from the tortured to the torturer; and from the unconscionable savagery of war and injustice to the daily struggles of those left desolate on our own inner city streeets, the poets echoed clearly and powerfully the indignation, heroism and hope that knows no borders. There could be no more fitting tribute to the Universal Declaration which so unequivocally sets out those rights to which all the citizens of the world are entitled.

Included with most poems was a letter from the author not just elucidating his or her work but expressing the honour they felt in being chosen to represent Amnesty

International and its work on behalf of human rights.

But inspiration, as all creative people know, is not enough, and we had little or no idea of how to go about publishing a book. Fortunately Marino Books shared our enthusiasm for this anthology. It was their interest, involvement and dedication that helped to turn our great idea into an even greater reality.

We extend our gratitude to all at Marino but especially to Jo O'Donoghue and Cormac Deane. Thanks also to Shaughn McGrath for his incisive and thoughtful cover graphics; Theo Dorgan and Niall MacMonagle for their invaluable assistance; and all at Amnesty International's Irish Section for their input and support. A special thanks to ColourBooks, who sponsored the printing of this book.

Finally, our warmest thanks to the poets of Ireland who so generously shared their work and their imagination.

Kenneth Morgan, Almut Schlepper
Ellen Dunleavy, Jacqueline Helme, Rachel Vaughan
Amnesty International Rathgar Group, Dublin
October 1998

Leland Bardwell

I have written a good few 'Prison Poems' and I feel that this one has the most universal touch.

The fact that time is both nothing and everything in prison is I hope encapsulated in this poem.

Prison Poem

Dawn lifts its blue-veined face
    slaps the chimney, slides down
    disappears beyond the kitchens.

Seagulls, fulmars, kittiwakes
    Freewheel for a frenzied dive.

Dawn has spoken, has cried,
    Kyow, kywow, kyawk.

Day shakes out its dirty shirt,
    Sleeves whisper, 'They've sold us down the river.'

Afternoon half rises, inert, polite.
    It soon is left for dead.

Night straps down its quilt
    Forces the colours behind our eyes.

We believe
    like children believe
    in the tall words of their picture book.

Sara Berkeley

I wrote this poem thinking of the stories I've read in Amnesty newsletters about occasions when letters from AI members have actually made their way into the prisoner's cell and revealed to them that the world knows and cares about their case.

As an Amnesty letter writer, I always hope that the letters I send will miraculously make their way into the hands of a person who will somehow be forced to do the right thing because of them.

The poem is also intended to say that the truth is stronger than prison walls.

A Thousand Letters

I dreamed you into my cell,
smelling of rain,
silvering the key in your palm,
beckoning.

The guards in their paper houses
sank me in here and I hit the stone
end of the well; ocean of hurt,
too much for one room.

What would I do with an ordinary day?
Out on the streets,
remembered blue of the dawn,
all roads lead to the sea.

A night's wind has softened the sand
but I leave no tracks, my thumbs bare
of prints, my photograph dissolved,
my bones erased.

The freedom is too thin, the dream frail,
the shadows escort me back,
there, at the end of fiction,
dawns an impenetrable light,

a letter from you, a thousand letters,
truth rises unobstructed,
bountiful and benevolent,
it winds white lilies around me.

Eavan Boland

This poem was written in the early Seventies, when random violence occurred often and a dark mistrust of speech and motive was beginning to be very apparent, even in the south of Ireland. I think any definition of human rights has to presuppose a common belief that people can continue to talk to each other across those barriers. But this is a poem about the distrust, not the aspiration. My sense of broken promises and of neighbourly trusts disintegrating was very real around that time.

The War Horse

This dry night, nothing unusual
About the clip, clop, casual

Iron of his shoes as he stamps death
Like a mint on the innocent coinage of earth.

I lift the window, watch the ambling feather
Of hock and fetlock, loosed from its daily tether

In the tinker camp on the Enniskerry Road,
Pass, his breath hissing, his snuffling head

Down. He is gone. No great harm is done.
Only a leaf of our laurel hedge is torn –

Of distant interest like a maimed limb,
Only a rose which now will never climb

The stone of our house, expendable, a mere
Line of defence against him, a volunteer

You might say, only a crocus its bulbous head
Blown from growth, one of the screamless dead.

But we, we are safe, our unformed fear
Of fierce commitment gone; why should we care

If a rose, a hedge, a crocus are uprooted
Like corpses, remote, crushed, mutilated?

He stumbles on like a rumour of war, huge,
Threatening; neighbours use the subterfuge

Of curtains; he stumbles down our short street
Thankfully passing us. I pause, wait,

Then to breathe relief lean on the sill
And for a second only my blood is still

With atavism. That rose he smashed frays
Ribboned across our hedge, recalling days

Of burned countryside, illicit braid:
A cause ruined before, a world betrayed.

Dermot Bolger

I have chosen 'Lines for an Unknown Uncle' because it seems to me that the person it was written about – an uncle who died from fever in Wexford early this century – represents all those millions of deaths that never make the news and soon become the forgotten minutiae of any age and time.

Stalin said that one death was a tragedy and a million deaths a statistic. My uncle died in no labour camp nor did he endure the man-made tortures that so many of Amnesty's campaigns are about. His death was a mundane event of the time, one of hundreds of thousands of children who died in slow agony. I had never heard of him until recently. My poem is simply an attempt to take his death from the cold statistics and make it real again.

Lines for an Unknown Uncle

No son or granddaughter to remember:
   No trace of your seventeen years left,
Except in the mind of a younger brother

   Sent out onto the street to wait,
While you screamed in the height of fever
   For someone to finish you with an axe.

Pat Boran

Here is a relatively recent poem. I'm never really sure how or when poems get started, but I could say that this one (commencing with the first two lines late one night, and then not returned to for months) began as an argument against the notion that we are all inherently dirty, creatures of earth whose spirits are merely trapped inside us for our mortal duration – a bizarre notion that is not only behind so much of western civilisation but that has been used by religions and governments over the millennia to justify murder, genocide, enslavement and, on almost every level of daily living, some form of oppression. Where the poem began to take on a life of its own, though, if indeed it has one, was where it expanded to take in not just these injustices on a global level but to deal with something that was part of my own immediate life. I am not saying that a poet must balance the public grief with his/her own private grief. That would be to deny that there are scales and levels of injustice. What I *am* saying is that a poem which somehow finds its way home, which somehow makes the connection between the enormous horror, or indeed beauty, of the outside world and its equivalent in the private domain, has far more chance of reaching that part of the psyche almost uniquely dependent on poetry for its news, perhaps the very part of the psyche that keeps us human.

Flesh

The spirit, despite bad press,
loves the flesh.

It enjoys nothing more
than body odour,

the warmth of a crotch
or the electric touch

of lips. Those dark religions
which have banned the nether regions

to the netherworld, to hell,
can cast all the spells

they like, can single out for blame
those who refuse to feel shame

about their bodies – children, the old,
the savage inhabitants of the Third World,

but most of all those women of loose morals
whose torture is somehow part of the quarrel

about sanctity and sin
and the vessels the soul is to be found in.

Enough idols and bones!
Enough gleaming chalices and altar stones!

I say it again: the spirit loves
the flesh, as the hand the glove.

And if you doubt me, ask my dying father
which he would rather:

to be done at last with love and pain,
or to leave, but then come back to flesh again.

Rory Brennan

Flicking through the books I have written (always a rueful task for a writer) for something that was consonant with the uplifting, ever-essential but nonetheless intimidating concept of Human Rights, I came up with this short piece from my first one, 'The Sea on Fire'. I do not know who I had in mind when I wrote 'Ballad of the Yes Man' twenty years ago; perhaps a still-living statesman of the Vietnam era, perhaps that old trickster Talleyrand, even the imperialist manipulator Lord Milner. Today the personality that most seems to fit – and pay – the bill is the loathsome Beria, Stalin's chief of police.

But the real yes man (or woman) is not an amalgam of historical figures; the yes person is every one of us as exemplified in the slippery line where compromise slides over into cowardice. We cannot pick up on every small slight or rant on about every tiny wrong; neither can we allow minor injustices to burgeon into huge ones. Then just where should we take a stand? The excruciating problem of human beings violating human rights is closely linked to how all of us live and make our decisions day in, day out.

Ballad of the Yes Man

His gift was to agree
With any ambivalent scheme,
Argument or theory.
'I am, therefore I seem'.

His version of events
Took in important statesmen
And refugees in tents.
He smiled on television.

When they tried to implement
His 'miracle' solution
The veil inside the temple rent
With the roar of revolution.

A neutral in a no man's land,
Shot at by either side,
He hid in a shell-hole and
Cowered till he died.

Heather Brett

This is a poem about injustices. And sometimes the only way to deal with injustice is to believe in an alternative ascendancy or justification over and above the actual.

The Man Who Crushed Butterflies

I have heard of your kind.
When we travelled by waterfall
from one land mass to the other,
my sodden shawl keeping my face frozen for centuries,
you were there, on each bank, prodding
with whittled saplings to keep us from landing,
to keep us moving.

And later, when we leased a landscape in our name
you came to isolate us
the sharp barbs, the boundaries well depicted in your
closed mind.
We said nothing, turned our attention to other things,
carried on learning, gleaning knowledge from the earth
and every living thing.
At times, even you.

But still you taunted us, shoved your opinions down
our throats
until we choked, the best of us yielding,
ending up in suburbs where indoctrination is being
taught all over again
or hospitals and asylums when the truth hurt.
You bit our hands, undermined us at every turn
gave us only the darkness to crawl into.
Only our thoughts were free.

And yet we hear you. Each night we wince
at your every howl, knowing we could've saved you.
Your bones are crumbling, your blood is turning to
sand.
We can't condone you, for on your palms
are the powdered remanents of vibrant colours
but we understand your pain.
Some kinds of peace will never be for you.

Paddy Bushe

I wrote this poem the day after a peace settlement was agreed by the parties in the North. While it is not clear as of now whether or not the public will vote in favour of the agreement, I wanted to celebrate and salute the 'nuts and bolts' aspects of human rights – the compromises and the hard slog of negotiation which are the other, necessary side of principle and ideology, and without which idealistic beliefs can degenerate into dogmatism and even tyranny.

Assemblage

Here is a new sculpture, not magnificently
bronze, nor pedestalled on granite.
This is tinkering, gathering, an assemblage.

Here is a bolt coaxed where it doesn't belong,
with exquisite care not to shear the thread.
Here are dirty hands, and coarse cleansing.

This is a sculpture of midnight phone-calls,
of walk-outs and re-draftings and strategies.
Here is the ache of many twisted arms.

This is a sculpture that has been spun
and doctored and bandaged and splinted.
Here are crutches, oils for hurt egos, cures.

Here are the disposable pens of civil servants
who rewrite tablets that we thought were made of
    stone.
Here are computers that move words like mountains.

Here are paramilitaries studying paragraphs
and parameters, paraphrasing what is paramount
for all the heads to stay above the parapet.

Here are the strands too complicated to follow,
and here are the weavers, honoured at last:
here are the politicians, really making shapes.

And the sculptors walk, amazed, around their work,
not sure of what to say, realising there's no need
for the statues they love to be cast in a furnace.

Louise C. Callaghan

This poem was written while I was away for a year living in Oakland, California. It is about resilience, human survival. Many young people have to leave their homes, flee their homes, leaving family and everything which is familiar behind, to find survival in a foreign country. This poem is a recognition of and a salute to their immense courage.

Paquida

The young black girl
hardly visible on my dark porch
again last night.

I asked her in.
She is seventeen –
lives in a shelter

came here a year ago
with her father:
The first person I've met

from Mississippi state,
though I learnt to spell it
when I was eight!

She stands to leave, we embrace:
'I been drinking' she says
'but, A'm still myself'.

Gust of a thousand winds
blew through me –
the dimming stars

gathered in the soft-black
folds of her skirt:
Ghost of a dream at dawn.

At her age, leaving home
nothing could reach me,
sad to the point of death.

Moya Cannon

'Going for Milk' was an attempt to explore the dynamics of fear – how fear begets fear which begets violence and of how risks must be taken to break this dynamic.

Going For Milk

Coming on the *Stop* sign at night
on the bend of a side road
I braked too fast,
too far from the barrier.

The soldier with the red torch
and the machine-gun
stepped back,
spoke to someone in the steel tower
then half-circled the southern car.
You'll be all right.
They won't do you a bit of harm if you don't scare them.

Every morning before school
I took the can,
crossed the road,
climbed a stile into McGarveys' field,
stepped down sideways from the bottom step
to avoid the mud
and turned a corner behind Barlows'
to where cows lifted their horns out of the long grass,
started to move in.

Keep on going, they are far more afraid of you
than you are of them.

The soldier at the car window has a helmet too big for
      him,
is barely an adult, seventeen, eighteen maybe,
younger than my nephew, smaller.
He smiles, in relief.

Who sent him out?
Who sent any of them out
telling them once more
absent mindedly, maybe,
turning off the TV or hanging a cup up on a hook,

They are all the same, that crowd,
trust none of them
they're all tarred with the same brush.

And who is going to tell them the truth
which is not simple
which sounds like the blackest lie
when they have stood
in a kitchen
where killing was done –

They're not all the same
most of them are far more afraid of you
than you are of them.

Be careful now,
go on over, the milk is badly needed.

Philip Casey

I wrote this poem in Dr Steeven's Hospital, Dublin, in 1983 – or more accurately, it came to me like a message from another realm. I can't remember how I was aware of the murders of Guatemalan Indians, but they were on my mind. It was late at night, and I was in pain and probably drugged to the gills, when I had a vision of fireflies coupled with a powerful sense of identification with the victims of the Guatemalan horror. Some years later, I had the moving experience of seeing the poem dramatized by Terry McDonagh and his cosmopolitan students at the Internationale Schule in Hamburg.

An Indian Dreams of the River

I can no longer smell freedom on the river.
A woman's life is always hard, but at least
I had my teeth, then. My smile was famous
in the village.
They have polluted my river with the burning leather
of their jackboots.
At night, when the fireflies eat my brain,
I think of how they broke my husband,
bone by white bone.
Curse by obscene curse they raped me,
clutching José's swollen eyelids open
to see our shame.
I cannot eat fish anymore because they remind
me of their eyes.
Sleep comes like a caravel of *conquistadores*,
gleaming Toledo bayonets flecked with blood

Patrick Chapman

The reason I think this poem is appropriate is that it was written on the fiftieth anniversary of the last time atomic weapons were used in war. However, the war has continued in the minds of people ever since. Even with the passing of the Cold War, the memories of a time when one thought every day: *is this going to be the day?* remain. I believe that it's a human right to live free of this fear as well as of others, and this right has been violated ever since 1945 simply by the existence of these weapons.

Deadbeat

9 August, 1995
Discovering its body
In the attic living room
Where, some nights before,
I'd trapped the moth ~

Forgetful of my acquiescence
To the darkness I'd unleashed
Inside its brain ~

I regarded with indifference
This un-generation,
Toying with a role for it:

'Moth, you were a bomber
Of dust-mite Nagasakis . . . '
And thought of *Little Boy, Fat Man,*
Their masculine nomenclature.

Sean Clarkin

I choose 'The Dissenting Voice' in tribute to all those who have ever redeemed mankind by choosing that path. I hope the 'Christian' or 'believer' element can be understood in the broadest sense. Certainly, belief and its tendency towards dogmatism fascinates and appals me. This piece was written at a time when darker forces were casting shadows even here in Ireland.

The Dissenting Voice

I fear now
As many do in South America
and elsewhere . . .
Many will not believe it
but I fear
the 'pop' in the night
the gun exploding
in the brain.

I cry to you, lord
Not in fear
lord
but on the edge of loneliness.

You have given me courage
lord
now still the fear.
What people will do
in your name
lord
I fear.
The hysteria that will be
indeed

is being
called your will . . . as so in
                    the past.

Restore peopleness
to those
from whom it is slipping
                    away
Let them not be moulded
even by your Priests, lord
into that awful oneness
that gave us Belsen and Treblinka.

Still the hearts
of your Ministers, lord
that they be not blasphemers,
Dogmatic where there is no
Dogma.

Let them walk down
the streets of our loneliness
and if they rise to their pulpits
go with them
with your longsuffering

If
we are driven
after long thought
towards the entrance marked
'Resist' and have souled
ourselves against the easy way
You must be with us too.

Harry Clifton

This poem ought to be self-explanatory, but it might be useful to know that the house – from which one of the residents was deported to a Nazi concentration camp in 1942 – is situated in a working-class, predominantly foreign suburb of Paris. The inferences – threat of expulsion in a closed society, not to mention the whole illusion of domestic permanence – are, I hope, somewhere in the background.

The House of the Deportee

Always in shadow, the house of the deportee
Was its own landmark
On the avenue. Groceries, carparks
Owed their lives to him, who was taken away,

Bewitching himself to a tree at his own front door,
And in April, the spores,
Like mattress ticking, feathers that flew,
Swarmed at the windows hindsight could see through.

Not that the house was empty. Upstairs light,
Diurnal time, and the shapes
Of daily living – sudden figures of eight
And vague daguerrotypes

From the age of black and white
Against the shades. November, and at night,
While the asphalt smoked
With rain and the sizzling wakes

Of passing cars, the immigrant quarter slept
Behind double locks, iron shutters.
There, where trading hours were never kept,
Where the laws were lived in spirit, not in letter,

Where brilliant elfachromes,
Household idylls, plastered the city gates,
They still remembered the man who got up from his
    plate
To answer a doorbell once, and never came home.

Michael Coady

Man's capacity for evil is a constant in the world, but human goodness is also an abiding reality. The inspirational outreach of the human spirit finds creative expression in all the arts, but perhaps most instinctively and universally in music.

Though There Are Torturers

Though there are torturers in the world
there are also musicians.

Though at this moment
men are screaming in prisons

there are jazzmen raising storms
of sensuous celebration

and orchestras releasing
glories of the spirit.

Though the image of God
is everywhere defiled

Mozart and Beethoven
forever bring us healing

a woman in west Clare
is playing the concertina

and a drunk man on the road
is singing for no reason.

Declan Collinge

This short poem describes the prisoner of conscience awaiting torture and execution, hearing for the last time the song of a bird in the distance. Just as the bird's note increases in volume when it joins the dawn chorus, so the chorus of protest increases in volume until it is an urgent carillon of bells heard throughout the world, transcending the sounds of torture. I am confident that this metaphor aptly describes the work of Amnesty and I am honoured to have been asked to contribute.

Chorus

In the grey distance
A bird sings above the seeping
Walls, its frail notes hesitant

As the mind, taut, awaiting
Shock imminence
Of flame or cattle prod:

The nails extracted
In the nightmare
Of a thousand cells

Scratch their red calligraphy
From station to station

As the bird's voice
Crescendos in chorus
Sharper than the ring of steel,

And the clear carillon of bells
Defies the dawn volley
Its growing insistence
Louder than injustice.

Roz Cowman

'Peanuts' was written around 1984. The title and contents refer to Charles Schultz's well-known cartoon series; I contrast the childhood of these children with my own childhood terrors in Ireland in the 1940s. If there is a conclusion to be drawn, it must be that children's rights to a full, human life are constantly violated.

Peanuts

The way it was, for us children
during the forties
in those narrow market towns,
cow-spattered curtain-twitching
tinker-crazed on fair-days,
and we picking our way though forests
of drunken giants' legs . . .

things should have turned out better
for Charlie Brown and Snoopy
roller-skating top-spinning
in backyard prairies of bungalows
down the broad sidewalks of America,
and all the giants invisible,
at work behind the scenes.

David Croft

'Any Name You Could Possibly Think Of' describes a visit to a First World War memorial in Edinburgh. Events of the war are so far back that they don't really affect us any more. Until you visit a place like the memorial which commemorates the millions of people who lost their lives. Then the futility and true enormity of the loss of human life really comes home.

Any Name You Could Possibly Think Of

I was reading a dusty old book
in the Edinburgh Castle War Memorial.
The book was as big as a table
and filled front to back
with thousands upon thousands of names.

Above the book was a shiny bronze plaque.
And above the plaque was a flag.
Fading regimental colours that,
even now, smelled of grease and blood.

I strolled around the sombre hall
tracing my finger down the cold metal grooves,
feeling the 'theatres' through half closed eyes:
Ypres, Gallipoli, Somme,
Flanders, Mons, Arras,
Jutland, Amiens, Baghdad . . .

Outside, I lit a cigarette,
and gazed over the battlements,
as the city disappeared
under a cold November mist.

'I bet,' I thought to myself,
'that any name you could possibly think of
would be in one of those books.'

Anthony Cronin

1798

Commissioned by Comóradh '98 to be read by the author on Vinegar Hill on 1 June 1998

They wore their Sunday best for early battle,
Coming with ribbons in their hats to join
Their neighbours at the crossroads by the chapel
As on a holy day of obligation.
War is release and sudden holiday,
For some, release now from a nightly horror,
The flaming thatch, the mingled oaths and screams.

The lovely summer weather gave them leave
To sleep beneath the bright and beckoning stars
And wake each day to Liberty's wide dawn.
But nothing happens as a wish would have it;
And war is chance, its currents rip us far
Beyond all headlands and all reach of rescue,
Beyond what heart can hope or soul can stomach.

Too soon the Slaney's waves were stained, the Barrow
Carried its cargo seawards from New Ross
To cold, wide waters where no sail appeared.
Their columns heaving now with frantic households,
Not heroes, merely people, but the pikes
Their hedge and shelter in the broken weather,
Here on this hill they stood, where we assemble,
A civic gathering in a different time.

History, the nightmare from which all mankind
Must struggle to awake, recedes at last;
And our normality accommodates
The dream of Liberty, Equality
For which they had to rend the normal day,
To take the lives of others, give their own;
What seemed so distant then, to us mundane.
We should recall the price they had to pay.

Leo Cullen

The View Above Rosenallis

I met them in their child pedal-cars at a cross-roads
on a hill at the edge of a wide plain.
I was admiring their hand-signals.
We're not very religious, he said
We used to go to Mass once,
for the little one's sake,
so she would have it.
And for the young lad before her.
Now neither of them go.
So we come up here.
For a Sunday drive.

They were elderly, he wore a hat.
Her face was creased with the pleasure of greeting me
in such an out of the way spot
From the roof of an old station-wagon he had taken
down two pedal-cars,
lead-painted, one blue, one green
and on the quiet cross-roads overlooking the plain
they pedalled by one another.
The only place you can still practise hand-signals,
he said.
A crowd of us will be whooping it up here in an hour
if you hang on.

The view of this plain is immense
I can see vast crossings of ancient tribes
soldiering home after war
dogs and baggage-animals behind,
women and children
pulling stick-trailers.
And on the edge of enmities,
where opposing factions will always mingle,
opposing tribespeople commercing:
trick o' the loop men,
three card tricksters,
tick-tack men,
handstand-artists.
And look,
at the edge of the bonfires,
jugglers, palm-readers.
All, what you might call, whooping it up.

Tony Curtis

I recently had the great privilege of hearing Palden Gyatso, a Tibetan monk who was imprisoned by the Chinese for thirty-three years, speak at the launch of his book 'Fire Under the Snow'. Listening to his story, I was deeply moved. He said that if he were to cut down every tree in Ireland and turn them into pencils and then use the sea around Ireland as ink, he would not have enough pencils nor enough ink to write of all the horror he has witnessed in his native Tibet, at the hands of the Chinese. As he told his story, he made the point that when he was adopted as a prisoner of conscience by Amnesty International the quality of his life greatly improved and for this he would be eternally grateful. Palden Gyatso's life improved enough that he has lived to be a voice for those who died.

My poem 'Still Life' comes from a story I heard about the thirteenth Dalai Lama. It seems that he spent ten years making a clock, finished it, wound it up and then hit it with a hammer, everything in his world being transient. This most patient understanding of life is strikingly expressed by the present Dalai Lama. I have heard him say that in time the Chinese will leave Tibet, as the Tibetans once left China. Let us hope so.

Still Life

When I heard of the Tibetan
who made a clock
and then destroyed it
because it would be
yet another distraction,

I wondered was he troubled
by the ticking?
Was he worried he'd never
be quite sure whether to place it
on a shelf or by the bed?
Maybe he felt he'd always
be getting up to glance
at its slowly changing face
or to settle the hands.

So why did he make the clock?
Was it to see if time moved?
And then – suddenly –
at the first tick, it did,
and he began to wonder:
How long do I work?
What's it take to walk from one
end of the valley to the other?
Does day pass quicker than night?

I can see him now, that quiet man,
stepping away from the table,
taking a deep, slow breath,
as he lifts the hammer and swings
so the cogs, and the ticking,
and the time, vanish in a moment.

Padraig Daly

The people of Chernobyl, who were affected so severely by nuclear fallout, are forgotten by most of the world. I wrote this poem after reading Adi Roche's account of her work with the Chernobyl children. Her generosity and that of her fellow workers are inspirational. She shows us how good people can make a difference.

After Chernobyl

The children refuse sweets,
Reject toys and picturebooks,
Are sick all day.

They do not understand what is happening to them:
Why they have been brought to this place,
Why their parents do not visit,
Why none of us appears before them without
      camouflage,
Why we do not touch or comfort them.

They miss the grumbling hens,
The flea-hassled dogs,
The irritable goats,
The wasps humming in the orchards,
The old people chattering before the houses

Meanwhile in the villages, those who remain
Shake off their clinging homes,
Cleave themselves free of their fields,
Climb lorries to uncertain futures,
Raise cries that pierce to God.

Gerald Dawe

I wrote this poem over two summers. It's about borders between everyday 'ordinary' life and how that can be invaded by political violence, such as ethnic cleansing. The poem is also about hope even when we're not quite sure of the direction we're heading in – 'a possible land', as MacNeice put it.

Summer Journal

for Brendan Kennelly

Through the porthole of a window
    the blue muggy night is perforated
with the sound of foghorns.
    Dogs answer each other back
and then it thunders again with spectacular effect.
    The girls are sleeping in the cool apartment;
shadows like 'planes cast over the lawn.
    I'm in two minds between *Tender is the Night*
and the tv's mute hectic images
    which flash worldwide with breaking news
of a hillside trek and scorched villages,
    the bedecked impromptu briefing.

The ignominious beetle covers oceans of sand
    but the man or woman who drifts
into the sky, paragliding over our prone bodies –
    family groups setting up makeshift home,
couples in their prime and past their prime,
    the odd one alone stretched under the sun
where all are vulnerable, torn this way
    and that, naked, flat, in repose from
the everyday, at sixes and sevens –
    is trussed and hooked to the speeding boat
and, cradled like a baby, looks down
    upon us all with far-seeing love and pity.

Palm doves and swallows in the apricot
    and oleander, the cacophony
of high season; poolside, *Mitteleuropa*
    tans and observes in silence a Galleon
take up the full of the Bay.
    The rosé goes down like mother's milk,
it's near ninety, best head for cover;
    in the shade local dance music
beats through the scratchy airwaves
    to you on whichever island you stand:
        'Let us dream it now,
    And pray for a possible land'.

Seamus Deane

I wrote this poem several years ago but never tried to publish it or some companion pieces that all had to do, one way or another, with the notion of the cancelled, buried lives that are part of the inevitable silent history of the modern state. It thus seems opportune to publish the poem now, under the aegis of Amnesty International, an organisation that has often broken that silence on behalf of the oppressed.

Buying Time

Most of the time I would be asking
Questions and getting nothing
Back. Like a child learning
To speak, I'd only a few sounds
For many things. There were times

When I'd point my voice like
A finger at something but all
That happened was that the globe
Kept on spinning, trees swayed
In their surf, the histories of people

Vanished at a stroke in auctions,
In choice words, in courts and prisons,
Or were left like a snapped key
In a lock, to be retrieved only as myth,
Legends in another's lifetime.

So, I stoked my wallet with hot
Unironed money that I used
To buy back their time; it was plural,
Cowering like refugees inside
The storm of the question,

Forgotten eyes lifting out of the dark
To be seen rather than to see
Past the bribed gaoler, the stifled
Report, the voice pointed here,
Quivering there, sailing close

To the wind that is now a slow air,
A woe pursued by sweetness, someone
Singing at a wedding as the rain falls
Like glass in the slanting forest
Where a tree has soundlessly gone down.

Celia de Fréine

I have chosen this poem because it tells the story of a woman who, in wartime, is faced with additional problems in finding food for her children. Her voice is that of one of the many nameless women whose story is usually told through word of mouth. To highlight this, I have juxtaposed her struggle to survive with that of a male formalist poet.

There Was a War On

This is how it happened. The bus
was trundling through the cindered city.
I had crossed the line to get provisions –
meat and veg, the kind of stuff you take
for granted, when just before the desert
we were held up by a couple of outlaws,
needing someone to make an example of.
There wasn't much to choose from –
me and a wan wimp of a poet. And, Gracie,
it wasn't the story of my life that flashed
before me, but a vision of his sonnets,
sestinas, villanelles, hurtling off a giant roll
of paper, the sort you see in the butcher's.
I'll go, he said to the guy
with the armalite, *this woman has kids.*

Bhí Cogadh ar Siúl

Seo mar a tharla. Bhí an bus ag treabhadh
tríd an chathair chrándóite, is mé tar éis
an líne a thrasnú ar thóir soláthairtí – feoil
agus glasraí, an sórt stuif a nglacann tusa
lena bheith i gcónaí sa chófra. Díreach
sular shroicheamar an fásach ionsaíodh sinn
ag cúpla meirleach a bhí ar lorg duine éicint
le heiseamláir a dhéanamh as. Ní raibh
de rogha acu ach mise nó file piteogach,
óg ach sách maith. Agus a Ghráinne, níorbh é
mo scéal féin a scinn os comhair mo shúl,
ach aisling dá dhánta díreacha, dánta grá
is aortha, iad ag léim de rolla ollmhór páipéir,
an sórt a fheictear i siopa an bhúistéara.
Rachaidh mise, ar seisean le fear
na harmailíte. *Tá gasúir ag an mbean seo.*

Greg Delanty

Some time ago I visited Sri Lanka and it struck me while there how its troubles are not too unlike the troubles on the island of Ireland. It is an island – about the same size as our own – that is an independent state now, but that was once ruled by England. There is a war going on between two economic, social and religious groups, the Sinhalese and Tamils, particularly in the northern part of the island. I have also read and heard how Sri Lanka is known as the Emerald Isle. Since everyone and everything seems to me to be a variant metaphor for everyone and everything else on some level, and that this seemed such a striking one I wrote this piece as a metaphor for the troubles in Ireland, thus the epigraph from Paul Muldoon and the various allusions within the poem to the poems of other poets writing about Northern Ireland.

The Emerald Isle

It's all much of a muchness.
Paul Muldoon, 'Aisling'

The machine gun-police chat at the temple's
    checkpoint,
    strafed by the confetti of bougainvillea
that's as common here as fuchsia on our own Emerald
        Isle.

They point out a Monitor basking in the foetor along
    the banks of Kandy's lake where men
were once staked to its floor for speaking out.

The lizard's charcoal body is patterned in links
    as if local gods chained the creature
into itself for some accurst, century's old aberration.

When these oddly convivial guards tell us that magic
    words flow from the tongue of
whoever touches the lizard's tongue, I could risk prayer

at the moated temple not for the gift of words for
    myself,
    but that the Tamils and
Sinhalese would risk talk, dumb and green as it sounds.

And fancying they've touched the flickering, forked
    tongue,
    this chevron of evil
would suddenly fan out into the victory sign of peace.

Louis de Paor

The forced separation of aboriginal children from their natural parents and their subsequent fostering by white families represents one of the most brutal and disgraceful aspects of Australia's colonial history. The title of the original poem in Irish translates literally as 'black into white' and is based on one man's experience of the 'White Australia' policy. In a documentary entitled *Black Magic* he tells how he was beaten when he resisted the legalised kidnap of his son, how he discovered his child's footprint in the red earth after the police had left and how he returned every day from then on to touch again the only trace that remained of his 'dead' son.

The image of a man touching the source of his own deepest hurt, refusing to accept the living death of his own flesh and blood seemed to me a poweful reversal of the encounter between doubting Thomas and the risen Christ. Coming from a supposedly Christian society it seemed a vicious irony that a perversion of the teachings of Christ should be used to justify the policy of assimilation on the basis that the children of indigenous parents would get a better upbringing among 'civilised' Christians. That an Australian Prime Minister should refuse to make an official apology to the 'stolen generation' during a recent national day of reconciliation suggests that the attitudes behind the attempt at a bloodless genocide have not yet been consigned to the dustbin of colonial history.

Assimilation

When the cops took his son
their bright batons left their mark
on his broken body,
the nails on their polished boots
pierced his skin.

When his loving hand uncovered
a child's footprint untouched
in the desecrated sand he heard
a highpitched scream sharp as a knife
gash the unprotected earth.

Day after day he hears
the scarred earth cry out
when he puts his hand
in that dry wound.

Still he doesn't believe.

An Dubh Ina Gheal

Nuair a d'fhuadaigh na póilíní a mhac
d'fhágadar rian a mbataí geala
ar a chabhail chéasta
is lorg a mbróg tairní
buailte ar a bholg brúite.

Nuair a nochtaigh a láimh mhuirneach
cosrian linbh gan smál
sa ghaineamh airgthe mhothaigh sé
caolghlór leanbaí, faobhar scine
ag réabadh chraiceann na talún.

Lá i ndiaidh lae ó shin
airíonn sé scréacha tinnis
ón gcré ghonta nuair a chuireann
sé a mhéar sa chréacht tirim.

Fós ní chreideann sé.

Katie Donovan

This poem describes the burning of Bridget Cleary in 1895 by her husband Michael. He apparently believed that she had been taken by the fairies, who had left a changeling in her place. It was said in the folk wisdom of those times that if you suspected your wife or child had been taken in such a manner, you should burn the changeling in order to have your loved one returned to you. The event took place in Tipperary, in Bridget's own house. I owe my knowledge of this story to the folklorist, Angela Bourke.

This story is a very powerful tale of injustice. Such events go on every day even now, over 100 years later. Violent and unjust acts are carried out upon innocent people whose killers and torturers invent some sort of pretext for these terrible acts.

As for Bridget Cleary, she might have been an independent-minded woman whom Michael couldn't boss around. She might have been dissatisfied with him for perfectly understandable reasons. We will never know. What we do know is that Michael was angry with her, and sought a poor excuse in order to get his own back.

Changeling

'Are you Bridget Cleary, my wife, in the name of God?'
– Michael Cleary, Tipperary, 1895

Another woman
grows inside me:
she curls her lip,
she talks back.
She uses my voice
for taunting,
to try and open his eye:
to see what's wrong.

He says I'm away
with the fairies,
he tells the neighbours
and they agree.
They sit in my kitchen,
goggle-eyed, waiting
for signs.
She won't give them
the satisfaction,
she says:
'Yes, Michael, I am away,
to the place
your mother used to go.'

I know, even as
I hear her say it,
I've pushed him too far,
lifted the skirt
on the thing
I'm not to name.
I'm weak enough –
though I'm wearing
my Sunday best,
never wanting them
to pity me –
I haven't much fight,
for all my rising words,
so when he flings me down
I can hardly say
my name, a lapse
that gives him the rope
to hang me;
the proof he needs
to show them
I'm a changeling.

That's when the fire
burns my face,
and they all watch him,
and I know I'm gone
and she's gone,
the woman
who came and did this
with my voice,
she's left me
a shell
to be torched,
my flesh crackling
in front
of my own hearth;

and him saying always
that I was gone,
I was away
with the fairies,
and putting
the hot flower
of the log
to my brow,
and all our neighbours
watching.

Theo Dorgan

Federico Garcia Lorca, the centenary of whose birth occurs this year, was murdered for being Federico Garcia Lorca. Not for his politics, or his sexuality, though these marked him out for his murderers. They could not bear the blunt fact of his existence, and so they killed him. This goes on, always and everywhere, as acts of love and kindness and generosity go on, and all of this is called being human.

It Goes On

i.m. Federico Garcia Lorca

It goes on, Federico, it goes on –
in the hearts of the functionaries
who despise the poor,
in the boots of the black-robed priest
who would crucify Christ for impertinence,
in the shop-steward breaking the strikers,
in the butcher with his dreams of Franco,
the journalist with his dreams of Stalin,
the investment specialist blank in his dream of gold.

The black horses knock sparks from the stone
in alleys and shaded laneways
and the poor tense in their sleep as the patrol goes by –
as the children in doorways in Santiago,
the hookers in doorways in Washington DC,
the glue-sniffing runaways in Dublin
and women all over the world as the bars shut
tense in their sleep, holding themselves close.
Always the cars at night, marked and unmarked.

It goes on, Federico, it goes on
and still the bone moon rises
on lovers walking an eternal street,
cascando somewhere from a darkened room,
a dog crossing at streetlights,
somebody whistling him home –
this too goes on and soon it will be morning
where the river sweeps everything into the sea.
It goes on, Federico, it goes on.

I wrote 'Homecoming' during the summer of 1996 after watching a television documentary about conditions in Russia during the Stalinist era. In the face of the suffering and injustice shown in the programme it seemed impossible to respond in words. Yet, one detail from the story of one woman – who had spent many years in the Gulags – seemed to sum up the nature of the suffering she, and many others like her, had experienced. She said, 'In the Gulags there were no mirrors.' (To deny someone their own image is to deny them their identity and all forms of subjugation pursue this end in one form or another.) In the poem I attempt to imagine the moment when she finally sees her face again; the moment when she has to attempt to understand herself again, if that is possible, after all she has been through.

I realise that this poem is an instance of the negative example – it is about the absence of freedom and its devastating effects on the individual made clear in a moment when freedom has been tentatively restored. What occurs in the absence of human freedom cannot be erased. It leaves an indelible mark like the scars this woman saw on her face in front of the mirror. Her story cannot be altered.

The poem is about one historical moment that is thankfully past. But history, it seems, repeats itself. This poem was not written for the occasion of this anthology. It was written for an occasion such as this; for a woman who I saw on television for a few moments whose name I do not know.

As the title of this anthology suggests, the response to human suffering cannot be delegated but is the concern of us all. It is our shared responsibility. I feel, therefore, both privileged and humbled to offer my poem as a contribution to this important book. I hope that in some small way it may help to promote the vital work done by your organisation.

Homecoming

In the Gulags, there were no mirrors.
Anonymous

Once said to have been as beautiful
as Comrade Stalin's bride,
she has returned to her home
in the village to find things
much the same as before
but covered now by a veil
of neglect and dust.

And like a schoolgirl complimented
for her looks, she runs
to her old room, to see
her face again in her grandmother's
gilded mirror above the bed:

she sees her mother's face
not her own, the fine features
blurred beyond recognition,
her nose broken, teeth rotten,
raven hair grey at the root.

And in the room she left
as a young woman, she chokes
to speak the altered syllables
of her name but cannot, wishes
every mirror in the world
smashed, blacked-out,
banished forever.

Oliver Dunne

'. . . peasants were shifted from the fields to factories . . .
The peasants slaved away to the point of exhaustion, but
now there was no one left in the fields to gather in the
harvest and, when crops — such as they were — failed again,
peasants began to collapse from hunger at their work.'

From *The Life & Times of Mao Tse-tung*

Death of the Renaissance

Statues heaped
in a deep grave

How funny red looks
on marble skin

Michelangelo
couldn't have carved that foot
better

Bend low,
you'll catch a human breath

Paul Durcan

Amnesty

I

The perimeter wall of a prison presents a problem
To a small boy,
Particularly if he is nine and a half
And he does not know, and nobody is ever going to
    tell him,
That when he was born, he was born in prison,
A confinement within a confinement.
Pardon? Pardon.

II

As he drives past the prison, Daddy does not explain –
'That's the prison.' If it was any place else
He'd spin around from the driving wheel and explain –
'That's the Rotunda Maternity Hospital'
Or 'That's the Wellington Monument'
Or 'That's the Four Courts.'

I swivel about in the back seat of the car,
A pair of small boy's eyes splattered all over the prison walls.
The prison is a blocked-up keyhole.
Its gates do not deign to speak to me.
They despise me.
Its barred cells do not deign to speak to me.
They despise me.
A grey, granite, waistcoated pile of sarcasm –
Like my arrogant, alcoholic big brother
The day he vomited into the fireplace.
Pardon? Pardon.

Each time we drive past the prison
– Which is four times a day –
I can see through its walls.
The prisoners' faces are decked out in vomit.
I am dejected that Daddy does not name it.

He who is the great namer of things;
For whom the names of places and people
Are the signs by which he teaches me
That they are holy and precious;
That the plankton of all human life is mercy.

Perhaps it is that a prison is not a holy and precious
    place –
A place that does not have a name.
Perhaps it is that prisoners are not holy and precious
    people –
People without names;
That the plankton of all human life is mercilessness.

III

I lie awake in bed at night fretting about the prison.
The headlights of passing cars toss shadows on the
    ceiling
That are cell bars. There are no faces.
But then the face of the Pope is projected onto the
    ceiling,
The Supreme Pontiff is appearing on the balcony of
    St Peter's.
I ask myself: When the Vicar of Christ's
Standing out there, explaining things to the world,
What does he make of the bars across his eyes?
How is it that I've never seen him put out his hands
And, falling to his knees,
Clench those bars fiercely, helplessly?
Yet Jesus is the patron saint of all prisoners

Because he was a prisoner himself,
Not a special-category prisoner
But a prisoner like the rest of us,
One of three.
Today you will be with me in paradise.
Pardon? Pardon.

Daddy puts his head around the bedroom door and
    whispers,
'Are you all right?'
I tell a lie and answer him:
'Yes, Daddy, I am all right.'
But I am not all right. The prison is all over the
    ceiling
And I am hiding from it down under the sheets.
The pink vomit of my big brother's sarcasm is all over
    my face.

IV

Against Daddy's wishes I courted a black girl,
A medical student from Cape Town.
'The most beautiful city in the world,' Daddy groaned,
Sobs of fury in his throat.
He put me out of the house and told me never to
    come home.
He loved me as no man ever loved his son
But he said to me – crisply, glassily, over the breakfast
    table,
Over the cornflakes and the marmalade – 'Don't ever
    come home again.'
Pardon? Pardon.

I went to another country and to a far place,
A mining village in northern Ontario,
A dark new habitat in oblivion,
And I freed myself from the dream of being his
    favourite son
And I found peace of mind in the company of my
    wife,
In the lovingkindness of her bed.
We have four boys and a girl, the youngest,
Whom we named Amnesty – after a radio programme
We'd heard, about people who write letters to
    prisoners.
It was the word, and the acoustic of the word:
Amnesty.
The etymology of the word:
Amnesty.
All participle, all verb;
Oblivion;
Like holding hands behind a waterfall;
Like a lake-dwelling on stilts in deciduous forests;
Like a nest caught up in a weir in a river in spate;
Like traffic lights at red when there's no traffic at
    night.

V

On winter nights when she's playing ice hockey on
    Main Street
I like to put my head out the door and call out her
name –
Amnesty.
It's so fortified, yet vulnerable, and it falls away
Or gathers itself to itself
Like a yard of deer bunching
In an open space at the tree line
Or between telegraph poles on a wet day.
'It's getting late, Amnesty, it's getting late.'

When I behold her racing back down the street to
greet me
What I feel is a sense of zero:
Amnesty.
It is such a swift and shedding spectacle to see her face
Peering out at me from its fur hood,
Its nimbus of expectancy with serrated edges,
All frills,
Oblivion,
And to hear myself reiterating her name –
Amnesty.

Pardon? Pardon.
It is such a delight to reiterate her name
– Amnesty –
That I cannot pronounce it often enough
– Amnesty –
And after we've made love
My wife puts me back down into sleep,
Oblivion,
By seashelling into my ear the lullaby of our daughter's
    name:
Amnesty
In the key of A minor
Into the seashell of my ear, the lullaby of my fate –
Amnesty.

Desmond Egan

While publishing a selection of my poems as 'Poems for Peace' in 1986 my publisher asked if I could write something on the theme of peace. As I tried to do so, it struck me that peace is as simple a thing as a walk down the road on a nice day – and yet, how few people in the world can enjoy such a luxury. So the poem has two moods. Seán MacBride wrote the introduction to my book and I dedicated the poem to him, as someone who had done so much for the cause of peace.

Peace

(for Seán MacBride)
just to go for a walk out the road
just that
under the deep trees
which whisper of peace

to break the bread of words
with someone passing
just that
four of us round a pram
and baby fingers asleep

just to join the harmony
the fields the blue everyday hills
the puddles of daylight and

you might hear a pheasant
echo through the woods
or plover may waver by
as the evening poises with a blackbird
on its table of hedge
just that

and here and there a gate
a bungalow's bright window
the smell of woodsmoke of lives

just that

but Sweet Christ that
is more than most of mankind can afford
with the globe still plaited in its own
crown of thorns

too many starving eyes
too many ancient children
squatting among flies
too many stockpiles of fear
too many dog jails too many generals
too many under torture by the impotent
screaming into the air we breathe

too many dreams stuck in money jams
too many mountains of butter selfishness
too many poor drowning in the streets
too many shantytowns on the outskirts of life

too many of us not sure what we want
so that we try to feed a habit for everything
until the ego puppets the militaries
mirror our own warring face

too little peace

Peter Fallon

In October 1992 I happily accepted an invitation to read my poems and lecture in Japan. I spent most of my time in Kyoto and much of the time there in the Zen gardens of that ancient city. These were interludes of extraordinary calm.

I've long cherished and sympathised with one of Eudora Welty's responses in an interview to a question about the causes she supported. 'Peace, education, conversation,' she said, before adding, 'and quiet'.

A world away, in the temple of Ryoan-ji, I sensed again that how we see the world is frequently a matter of choice, as is how we live in it.

World Peace

Cherries like ours
on their cherry tree.

Rock islands
in a gravel sea.

Ryōan-ji Temple, Kyoto

Gabriel Fitzmaurice

There's a story from Greek mythology about Zeus coming to a city and being refused hospitality there. He destroys the city in anger. In similar circumstances, Christ just walks away brushing the dust of the city from his feet. What we do to the least of his brethren, we do to him.

I let the tinker man be 'hunted' (as we say in north Kerry) from my yard. I don't blame the policeman. He was protecting the village, doing his duty, being prudent. That's the policeman's lot. The poet's is different. The poet is called to sympathise with all creation. And, on this occasion, I reneged. *Mea Culpa*. This poem is in penance for my sin.

The Day Christ Came to Moyvane

He came to fix umbrellas,
Kettles, basins, pans;
The squad car turned in my yard
And jumped the tinker man –

'What are you doing?', 'What's your name?',
'Get going out of here';
The tinker man walked down the drive,
My dog snapped at his heels.

But the tinker man was used to dogs,
He just kept walking on,
And as he walked he whistled
And was gone.

The Guard was doing his duty –
There had been reports
Of travellers casing houses.
I'd been robbed before,

So I thanked the Guard and offered him
A beer, a cup of tea,
And as we talked, the tinker man
Walked farther away from me.

Michael Gorman

Ronald Reagan came to Galway to receive an honorary degree at UCG. In the proximity of overbearing power I retreated to an early memory. I was five years old, my sister was four, we were walking home from school together, looking out for each other. I like to think that in each of the emperor's warriors there is a potential place that the emperor cannot reach.

In the Free World

No, we are not finally called home.
When we get out of this
Particular neck of the woods,
There is nothing on the other side,
Not the parents of Monsignor de Brun,
The ex-members of the Artane boys' band
Or a single representative from Taiwan.

Each year we become less.
We anticipate the deaths to come
Of those we truly love.
Will they be relayed by telephone
Or, personally, face-to-face?
Inadvertently, from a stranger's mouth?
Once or twice, perhaps, in letters?

For the umpteenth time, a voice
On the television is saying
'Here he is, the most powerful
Man in the Western World.'
And the omnipresent attaché case.
Overhead, the helicopters are whirring.
The manholes have all been checked.

I am losing contact with
Even the innermost things.

The day we were released early
From Doonally infant school
One of the teachers had gone to the well.
We walked home under trees.
The light played marvellous tricks
Along the clayey path.
The sun shone through, between
The moving leaves, et cetera,
Catching the puddles underneath.
Oh, to be in Doonaree
With the sweetheart I once knew.
I held my sister's small hand
Not wanting to reach the main road.

Kerry Hardie

This poem was written during the violent break-up of the
territories of the former Yugoslavia. It reflects the onlooker's
pain at the bloody upheaval and her sudden acute awareness
of the particularity and beauty of a landscape in time of
peace.

We Change the Map

This new map, unrolled, smoothed
seems innocent as the one we have discarded,
impersonal as the clocks in rows
along the upper border, showing time-zones.

The colours are pale and clear, the contours
crisp, decisive, keeping order.
The new names, lettered firmly, lie quite still
within the boundaries that the wars spill over.

It is the times.

I have been always one for paths myself.
The mole's view. Paths and small roads and the next
    bend.
Arched trees tunnelling to a coin of light.
No overview, no sense of what lies where.

Pinning up maps now, pinning my attention,
I cannot hold whole countries in my mind,
nor recognise their borders.

These days I want to trace
the shape of every townland in this valley;
name families; count trees, walls, cattle, gable-ends
smoke-soft and tender in the near blue distance.

Michael Hartnett

A Prayer for Sleep

Grant me good rest tonight, O Lord;
let no creatures prowl
the tangled pathways in my skull;
wipe all wars,
throw Guilt a bone;
let me dream, if I dream at all,
no child of Yours has come to harm.
    I know, of course, that Death's the norm,
    that there are people who have yet to climb
    the Present's rungs, who lag behind
    (hyaenas at the rim of civilisation's light)
    whose laughing hides a Stone Age howl,
    who wait, till darkness comes, to pounce
    and tear the guts of progress out.

Yet, grant me good rest tonight, my Lord,
blind my internal eyes;
guard my anxious, baffled years
with Your protecting arm
and let me dream, if I dream at all,
no child of Yours has come to harm.

Anne Haverty

When I saw a photograph of an old woman in Yeltsin's Russia doing what the poem describes, washing clothes on the bank of, I think, the Neva, I was struck by the helplessness of an ordinary life in the face of vast political abstractions. She had lived through two revolutions, communist and capitalist, which promised her so much but had failed to satisfy the small humble dream that would free her from one of her tougher daily chores.

She Dreamed of a Washing Machine

Look at her. A poignant lesson in revolutionary
    endeavour.
On her old knees in frozen mud on the bank of the
    river,
A glazed kerchief printing out her cold deaf ears – had
A fur hat once but Boris took it when he went to
    Siberia –
In a hole she's made in the ice, rinsing her grandchild's
    cottons,
Her fingers red as wheaty puddings dyed in cochineal.

And to think she used to dream of a washing machine.
One Spring lately, with a dollar she found in the street,
    she
Bought distemper and washed the common hall in her
    building
Lettuce green. But it needs a good scrub again –
A bit of soap and a lump of sausage this winter's
    dream.

At full tilt they passed her by, two revolutions already.
Like bright clouds in an April sky, spattering words,
Their words for her. To her they were all the one
    master,
The millennium upon her, she's hungrier and colder
And labours more than her own babushka she can
    vaguely
Remember, who was born in eighteen seventy four.

Dermot Healy

I choose this poem because Chris Abani, who spent some time as a political prisoner in Nigeria, liked it.

My House is Tiny

My house is tiny
And my sorrow
Is the smallest
At this end of the country.

And yet the whole sea
At my back
Can fit into
The most frightened

Human mind.

From the Republic of Conscience

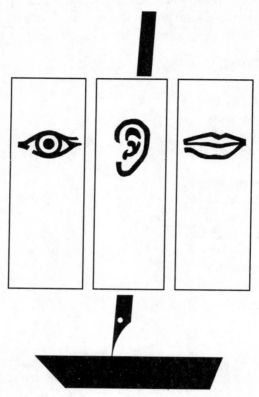

Written to commemorate the
25th Anniversary of
Amnesty International

by

SEAMUS HEANEY

Presented to each delegate at the
1989 International Council Meeting of
AMNESTY INTERNATIONAL
Dublin, Ireland

Seamus Heaney

From the Republic of Conscience

Written to commemorate the 25th Anniversary of Amnesty International and presented to each delegate at the 1989 International Council Meeting of Amnesty International, Dublin.

I

When I landed in the republic of conscience
it was so noiseless when the engines stopped
I could hear a curlew high above the runway.

At immigration the clerk was an old man
who produced a wallet from his homespun coat
and showed me a photograph of my grandfather.

The woman in customs asked me to declare
the words of our traditional cures and charms
to heal dumbness and avert the evil eye.

No porter. No interpreter. No taxi.
You carried what you had to and very soon
your symptoms of creeping privilege disappeared.

II

Fog is a dreaded omen there but lightning
spells universal good and parents hang
swaddled infants in trees during thunderstorms.

Salt is their precious mineral. And seashells
are held to the ear during births and funerals.
The base of all inks and pigments is seawater.

Their sacred symbol is a stylized boat.
The sail is an ear, the mast a sloping pen,
the hull a mouth-shape, the keel an open eye.

At their inauguration, public leaders
must swear to uphold unwritten law and weep
to atone for their presumption to hold office –

and to affirm their faith that all life sprang
from salt in tears which the sky-god wept
after he dreamt his solitude was endless.

III

I came back from that frugal republic
with my two arms the one length, the customs woman
having insisted my allowance was myself.

The old man rose and gazed into my face
and said that was official recognition
that I was now a dual citizen.

He therefore desired me when I got home
to consider myself a representative
and to speak on their behalf in my own tongue.

Their embassies, he said, were everywhere
but operated independently
and no ambassador would ever be relieved.

Michael D. Higgins

'Between Seasons' was written in 1997–8 at a time when I perceived a very corrosive rise in individualism representing a danger to many of the movements and organisations I had supported in different parts of the world. Nevertheless, it concludes after a bleak discourse with an assertion of there being a space of transcendent values – that we might call humanity.

Between Seasons

There is a darkness coming
That carries no
moisture
for a beckoning light.
It is a dry darkness
that threatens
of an arid time.

There are no words
sufficient
to rekindle a fire
of the senses.

It is a silence
that greets the dark,
where shadows of
things past,
flit past each other
haunting memory
As breath shortens
In the lifeless time.

And in the airless time
A great sigh breaks
Out of an endless longing.

It aches for a new
Beginning,
For a word,
for love
for hope.

When the silence breaks
Screams fill the air
and quiet prayers too
Directed at a God
Who remains
As silent as a blasted oak.
Screams and prayers
Draw no answer
From the dry air.

And in that time
inescapable
when planets die
There will be no sign
of an old time
of words.
All will have returned
to a dust
From which they came.

In these moments of half
light
We should not be afraid
to weep
at the coming darkness.

And from that moisture of tears
will spring the vivid flashes
of the senses
that allow us to dream
of a shared space

of humanity
In the time allowed.

It will come to be
that in the shadows
the breathless ones
will search for each other
weeping for the lost
words of love
not formed
in the time of
changing seasons.
Making an unbearable sadness
In the inescapable darkness.

But in the half light let us sing
In celebration
and weep too
in honesty
for the lost words
not formed,
the love not ripened,
the withered palm
not filled with chaff or seed.

We are waiting
between seasons.
The arid time beckons
And the beauty of the ordinary
Becomes precious
No flowers bloom
As we gaze in wonder
At a weed.

For in the roots of weeds now remembered
In our wait
Between seasons

are lodged
no mere dust
but seeds of beauty
scattered
on the thin soil of hope
that might survive
the airless time.

And no one knows
If it will ever be told,
nor will it matter,
in infinite space
That we made a story
With arrogant reason
In unbroken time.

That in the end
We yearned for hope
And a new place
Of spirit breath.

That in that place of Spirit
New life might come again
to play a new game
with mind and words.
That is our prayer
On the edge of darkness.

It is no void
but a space of infinite love
that waits
beyond the darkness.

Our final prayer
Poured . . .
Into the
Welcoming silence.

Fred Johnston

This poem is based loosely on Gaelic verse structure as a lament; poems of this sort written by Gaelic poets who found themselves oppressed or having to flee for their lives were common in the seventeenth and eighteenth centuries. I have tried roughly to imitate the pulse of this old Gaelic poetry which, as you know, was often a vehicle for protest and satire and political comment.

I have been particularly moved by the troubles in Algeria, a country I lived in in the very early Eighties. I am concerned that poetry itself can do nothing against oppression; that the act of writing poetry, particularly in a comfortable country such as our own, loses its force. I often feel that, when I'm writing a poem, it has no value when gauged against the world's tyrannies. The poem should be doing more – but what can it do?

We are comfortable, after all, over here – how do we view our poetry? What is its function?

I have tried in the poem to express the idea that there is considerable power in words, even though, as writers, we are sometimes hesitant, even fearful, about using our words to speak out against injustice. I think writers have a duty to speak out that is part of the reponsibility of their art. I'm sure not everyone would agree with me.

The Poet Laments the Uselessness of his Verse

Lodged in my cave of poetry
I did not hear the world's turning:

Looking out over the world
I did not see its toil below me.

Pity the scribe who has nothing
To compose upon but his poor self;

How like a noose to bind him
Is the bright circle drawn around him!

Often I have envied men who made
Words do more than rhyme and sing.

I have envied them and known
That I would not put myself out for them.

Pity the wordsmith who hammers
On the loud emptiness of his verses!

With a nail scratching on a stone wall
Other men inscribe words to shake a world.

In my airless cell of learning
I bend to the calm white empty page.

The sun hisses out in the empty ocean;
A dark doubt snuffs out the candle of poetry.

I have wasted words as if I had
A deep purse of them full forever.

Better for me to have chosen
One word to say each day of my life;

To have put that word in the mouths
Of men who could not speak for themselves.

Pity the poet whose verse
Has neither flesh nor bone:

Who comes to weigh his words
And finds them light as a feather!

Better to have written
One word that fed the heart

Than a lifetime's verses
Full of self-regard and philosophy.

Pity the rhymer who sings
Only the sound of his own voice.

Fergal Keane

This is a poem I wrote after the Rwandan genocide. During the genocide I came across a massacre of Tutsi villagers at a place called Nyarubuye in southwest Rwanda. I would like to dedicate the verse to the memory of all victims of genocide.

Just the Facts

Near the diocesan offices, 200 bodies, partially decomposed.
By the latrines, a boy, decapitated.
In a classroom, a woman and three children, decomposing.
Inside the church, a man, arms outstretched, rigor mortis.
Near the altar, boy, face down, maggots at work.
In another room, thirty or so bodies, blood on the walls.

Tell me, is smell a fact?
If it is, please record the following:
Rotting flesh, two to three weeks old.
A smell to draw flies, to call wild dogs, to charm rats.

I smelt something like it once when a truckload of offal passed down MacCurtain Street.
It was a hot day at the end of July, a day for Fountainstown beach and not the city.
I was a summer waiter in the Metropole Hotel, idling by the door when the truck passed.
Nothing made me hate that city life, made me yearn for salt water, as much as that smell.
Rotting, choking, puking. A smell with no future to it.

But I digress.
Back to the facts.
Total number of dead:
Approximately one thousand.
Manner of death:
Violent.

We stank for weeks.
The worst kind of smell.
A smell in the brain.

When I came back a year later,
the bodies were gone.

Until one night the rains came,
and the topsoil vanished,
and a child's small thighbone,
lay clean and white on
the sacred earth.

Anne Le Marquand Hartigan

I wrote 'Dear Life' in white heat a few days before the Gulf War, on hearing that Saddam Hussein had said it would be a mother of battles, adding horribly to the insult. The poem is a cry against war. Wars impose borders, are caused by fear of borders. War invades borders, denies human rights and takes freedoms away. Motherhood is never for war, but for hope and life.

Dear Life

A reponse to Sadam Hussein's obscene statement that the Gulf War would be a 'mother of battles'

Mother of Battles!
How dare you call us that!
I spit on you.
I am mother of children
pressed out in pain
from between my thighs.

You –
you were born thus,
give thanks.

How dare you call your evil mother.
How dare you spread your war lust on us.

Mothers, lovers, women, wives
Oh sisters my sisters shout cry
scream rage, all women all daughters
we love life, use your hands
to shelter small creatures.

What use is a lover
brought to me as a lump of meat on a plate?

I am helpless in my anger,
anger that flushes
for dear life,

our dear dear lives,
we have one only –

we have but one time –

this time
this day
this week
this minute

it is precious
and simple.

Save it
hold it
use it
love it

but destroy it not.

War
we are done with it
it is finished
we are grown up!
We won't say 'bang bang'

I would kick the man from my bed
that has war in his heart.

What is the use
in the song of blood?
What is the use of
splattered guts in the doorway?

Sit down sit down sit down
will you ever come here a minute
there is time –
if you will only let it be,

Breathe
there on the sand, breathe.
Take one word
used and dirty as it is –
how can I dare use it, but words are the tools I carry.

Peace

sound it,
as a breeze after long heat,
as the ease of a sweet kiss,
as the rain on the roof,
as breath from the nostrils of cattle,
in and out, in and out.

Does not the same sun shine on us?
Does not the same rain
give us drink?
Is not the world lying quiet in our arms?
Does it not shelter us?
Does it not feed us?
Is it not the promised land?

It is ours to plough
It is ours to reap
The earth has patience
and turns time slowly.

You are arrogant as mythical beasts
and as obsolete, out of date
Snorting over your disgusting pride,

Snorting over ownership
Snorting over power.

Give birth to one child –

The same sun rises over you Hussein.
The same moon sets over you Mr Bush.

Throw away greed
Throw away pride
We are brother and sister,

                    death comes to all of us
                    and it can come with kindness
                    when the wheel turns
                    at its own pace,

Do not insult us
with Mother of Battles.

We mother no war
no death
no hate
no rape
no torture
no obscenity of killings.
It is Father of Battles.
You rout like rutting bulls
brains a thick bone
your senses lost
in your snorts of pride.

Oh Arabians
ancient and proud
fingering the intricacies of culture

Oh Americans

young and brash
full of vigour and energy –
sit down will you –

sit sit down on the ancient desert
or beside the mountains of America
or by a sweet river in Europe
(all these gifts for living we have,)
and look, look on all that has been made.
Admit you do not understand.

You risk the world
for a little swagger,
you risk the world
for a barrel of oil.

Step away
step away from times past,
from old days when you rushed in to fight.

Those days are gone.
The world is trusting us,
the earth puts her head in our lap.
The child holds out a hand,
the woman closes the door, and waits.

We want a different landscape,
direct, as a child's drawing,

with the sun
still rising in the right hand corner,
and the moon
quieting us with silver light.

Michael Longley

In August 1994 I worked on the episode in Book XXIV of the *Iliad* where King Priam is looking down from the ramparts of Troy on to the plain below. There Achilles has killed his son Hector in combat. Not content with that, in his slow-burning rage Achilles drags Hector's corpse after his chariot. He mutilates it. Priam can stand this no longer. Though he is old and frail he visits the camp of Achilles to beg for Hector's body and for time to organise a proper funeral. It is a heart-stopping scene in which the balance of power gradually shifts from the great warrior to the old king. When he grabs his knees in supplication Priam reminds Achilles of his own ageing father, and the two men weep together. Achilles himself supervises the washing and wrapping of the corpse so that Priam won't have to see it. They're both emotionally drained by this time, so Achilles invites his old adversary to eat with him. I concentrated into a sonnet all that I wanted to borrow from this episode. Because at that time we were praying for an IRA ceasefire, I called the poem 'Ceasefire' and, hoping to make my own minute contribution, sent it to *The Irish Times*. It was the poem's good luck to be published two days after the IRA's declaration. Almost always a poem makes its occasion in private. This was an exception, and I still find warming the response of several readers, some of them damaged or bereaved in the Troubles.

Ceasefire

I
Put in mind of his own father and moved to tears
Achilles took him by the hand and pushed the old king
Gently away, but Priam curled up at his feet and
Wept with him until their sadness filled the building.

II

Taking Hector's corpse into his own hands Achilles
Made sure it was washed and, for the old king's sake,
Laid out in uniform, ready for Priam to carry
Wrapped like a present home to Troy at daybreak.

III

When they had eaten together, it pleased them both
To stare at each other's beauty as lovers might –
Achilles built like a god, Priam good-looking still
And full of conversation, who earlier had sighed:

IV

'I get down on my knees and do what must be done
And kiss Achilles' hand, the killer of my son.'

Since August 1994 I have read 'Ceasefire' many times in
public. But only once or twice have I pointed out that in
the *Iliad* the truce is temporary, that after the ceasefire the
Trojan War is resumed and Achilles himself is killed. I
suppose I was trying not to tempt fate. I did certainly have
misgivings. In my poem as in my political attitude, was I
pressurising those who had been bereaved or maimed to
forgive before they were ready to forgive? Was I in my
presumption suggesting that widows, widowers, orphans
might kiss the hands (as it were) of self-appointed murderers
and torturers? I was also sickened by the so-called
punishment beatings – hundreds of them. So in order to
challenge the symmetry of 'Ceasefire', I wrote a lopsided
eleven-line poem – an amplification, a qualification. The
new poem (on following page) is called 'All of These
People'.

All of These People

Who was it who suggested that the opposite of war
Is not so much peace as civilisation? He knew
Our assassinated Catholic greengrocer who died
At Christmas in the arms of our Methodist minister,
And our ice-cream man whose continuing requiem
Is the twenty-one flavours children have by heart.
Our cobbler mends shoes for everybody; our butcher
Blends into his best sausages leeks, garlic, honey;
Our corner-shop sells everything from bread to
    kindling.
Who can bring peace to people who are not civilised?
All of these people, alive or dead, are civilised.

Brian Lynch

Three Pieces in the Form of a Pair

1 Civilization

Manslaughter
Man's laughter

2 History

And with only an apostrophe
And a space between.

A possessive belonging to
Not an inch.

3 Human Rights

Not an inch
Either to the right
Or to the left.

But here now
In the middle of the silence
And the white space
A small voice:

The idea,
Immeasurable, of
You.

Joan McBreen

When the body of Aonghus Murphy was brought back to Ireland for burial in August 1986, there were many emotional scenes of grief, both public and private. The funeral service in the Cathedral of the archdiocese of Tuam was both an occasion of state solemnity and private family dignity. I wrote this poem in response to what I felt watching his parents, family and young fiancée, Martina Rhatigan, try to make sense of the cruelty and horror of war and its effect on the dreams and lives of the good, brave, young and innocent.

The Peace-Keeper

Dedicated to the memory of Aonghus Murphy, killed on active service with the Unifil troops in the Lebanon, August 1986.

The soldier's
dark-haired girl
had never seen

the scorching
Lebanon
sun

beat
its furious heat
on the yellow hills.

She did not hear
the screech
or flap

of frightened birds
or see them
fly

senseless
in the smoke-filled
sky.

She did not hear
the soldiers
there

curse and swear
before
they filled

the humid foreign
air
with cries.

And when
her peace-keeper's body
came home

no coolin airs
or purple-heathered
August haze

over brown
midland bogs
softened
the treachery.

No Army dirge,
or flags at half-mast
in silent
towns,

no sympathy,
or priest's gentle words
could change

her lament to lullaby,
or keen
him

ever from the damp
sea-salted
Galway soil.

Catherine Phil MacCarthy

The poem is dedicated to Lucy Partington, a student of Classics at Exeter University, who disappeared without trace one weekend in 1973, three days before her 21st birthday. Her bones were recovered and returned to her family in 1994 (during the trial of Frederick and Rosemary West).

I have chosen this poem in particular because it is a lament for the murder of a woman, and because it enacts her delivery from the place of violation, to a place of safety and peace.

Lucy's Song

for Lucy Partington

Uncover my bones, long dead and clean,
The moon of my skull that gleams in the mire,
Hold me to your breast, carry me unseen

From this vile place, where I have been
Dismembered for years, a brutal lair,
Uncover my bones, long dead and clean.

Blood of my blood, this is no time to keen,
Work by the colour of the dawn air,
Hold me to your breast, carry me unseen.

From the mouth of hell, unthread my spine,
Rib cage, pelvis, sacrum, in order,
Uncover my bones, long dead and clean.

From a chest of oak, let goodness shine,
A jar of honey, music of a choir,
Hold me to your breast, carry me unseen.

Sister, my sister, your love is mine,
I move with you, the silence is clear,
Uncover my bones, long dead and clean,
Hold me to your breast, carry me unseen.

Steve MacDonogh

Sometimes, paradoxically, we may gain a larger sense of the human universe as it is when we make of the present the past and of the past the present, and occupy for a moment a world before humanity.

Com an Áir

At the Bar law rested uneasily
on foundations of colonial precedent.
Cabinets relied upon the permanence
of a declared State of Emergency.
But before this, a story of blood and silence.

There is a clinging taste in the mouth
of earth, of things about to be born.
Turf-brown rivers run slow across the plateau
before cascading at the lip of the ridge.
Pinguicula's violet flower wears
a green collar shaped like a star,
littered with dark jewels of prey.

The civil servant toyed idly with a signet ring
and outlined environmental implications
of the enforcement of EC guidelines.
On a building site a sharp Northern voice
carried from the office a passionate demand
for the observance of a safety regulations.

Before this, a mountain track imitates
a river-bed bordered by turf banks
from which an ancient halberd protrudes
and multitudes of sharpened sticks of yew.
The shape of our history lies nascent:
if I penetrate the blanket bog

can I see the first farmers
begin to move up from the coasts,
along the rivers, above the tree-line
and into the peneplain resounding
to the generator hum of the wind
at Bearna na Gaoithe, the lofty
croak of raven, screech of falcon?

The cattle man shifted his cap back
with a thumb that paused at his lip,
adjusted his stance to the state of negotiations.

A history still unshaped, a story:
cattle like the black Kerry cow and,
equally small, the horses
move along the high valley
to the crossing points
of the mountains' spine.
It is a movement before nations,
before the name of Ireland.
There is no shade here,
nothing grows above knee height,
and even ten miles in the distance
the golden sweep of the bay
describes the bare shore
of a yet unpeopled sea.

Medbh McGuckian

The original subject of this piece was to register my acute sense of shock on discovering that one of the prisoners in my poetry session at Long Kesh was undergoing four life-sentences but was in fact innocent. Ten years of his life cannot be returned to him, and he is one of many, even though their release may come soon. I send it also on behalf of Róisín McAliskey, who was detained uncharged while her child was born under penal circumstances no less unjust than Anne Devlin's in 1803. Like her, she will bear the scars always. For those on death row, mostly blacks and some women, under federal law in several American states, where execution is a Damoclean sword. I hoped the chemical mix of the poem might hold a lot of ambivalent moral questions and responses in its solution.

Red Trial

I wanted to buy a man made from sleep:
an underground man, a new glittering iceberg.
But his perilous eight-ninths was so over-alive,
when I tried to interview the ever-present dead,
I wanted the truth and all I got was his body.

Close-lipped and stern, a mere husk, in convict
clothing; with an air of looking back on a love-
affair; actor with a single line, framing sentences,
sitting tensely forward in a pistol-point of time,
so all you could kiss was his finger-tips.

A letter addressed would almost certainly reach
his half-an-hour away, H-for-Henry, Tudor-shaped
end house: whose invisible fourth wall was
the whole world watching – a keyhole to which
an eye of every age was pasted.

The radio, that fair-faced conspirator, purred
with a positive belongingness, whispered
his name in Irish, wished to touch him where
a bill of dark particulars, black with one white
glove, hung like an act in the living-room.

'The defendant must have flown during a redundant
winter, when no planes landed, to a burned-down
    hotel.'
As if last January were standing floodlit, after
a long detention on mere suspicion, free to be silent,
entitled to a hearing, on an autumn day in court.

While sour soldiers, overgrown boys, met summer
half-way in their fall ensemble. What he had 'done'
had a winter-smell of mice and old wood;
its enormity dazed me like a sunburst, marking
his inmost bloom with a blunt malice

to a pirate flower curiously streaked,
though it is the hand holding it that is cracked
and seamed, by its power to harbour him –
the sea in labour every fifteen minutes
against what it should host, the all-night diver.

Derek Mahon

Kinsale

The kind of rain we knew is a thing of the past –
deep-delving, dark, deliberate you would say,
browsing on spire and bogland; but today
our sky-blue slates are steaming in the sun,
our yachts tinkling and dancing in the bay
like race-horses. We contemplate at last
shining windows, a future forbidden to no-one.

Paula Meehan

I wrote this poem when I lived in Fatima Mansions in Dublin's south inner city in the mid Eighties. I began to realise that indeed human rights do have borders and within the same city some citizens had more rights than others, whatever it says in the constitution. It was the gap between the aspirations of our republic and the reality of the lives around me that invoked the poem. I was also afraid of my own sense of being paralysed, of succumbing to a kind of ghettoization.

Those Nights

Fatima Mansions, Dublin, 1985

Those nights without bread, without coal,
When I rake up butts for a smoke
And stumble in the white space between stanzas,
I need you least, having nothing to give.

Those nights, starry and cold, I belong
With the mad, the chipped, the lumpen
Tatterdemalions wheeling, duped by the light.
I do not begrudge you your wholeness.

Those nights when the tide song is trapped
In the shell, and men with drawn batons
Mass in the street, their eyes void of pity,
I do not disturb you. I leave you be.

On those nights when the wounded street
Will not heal and words are rooks
Randomly tangling in clusters in my head,
I do not envy your peace. You are innocent.

Noel Monahan

I feel that this poem is representative of the opposites that haunt our lives. The two buildings stand like dragons on opposite sides of the street as we celebrate Christmas and peace.

The Same Child

Here we are again
In our separate places,
You in the finery of your stained glass
And me with my Graeco-Roman look

On Christmas night. Inside
We both house the same child
Destined for the same cross
And the one star lights us up,

While we stand our ground
Gazing at each other,
On opposite sides of the road
In an Ulster town, in the South.

John Montague

Last year, my companion and I travelled to Okinawa, a small island with a largely tragic history. I had been asked to speak at a university on the similarities between Ireland and Okinawa, both island nations which have had to contend with a larger, powerful neighbour.

In the course of our journey we were brought to a museum which commemorates a group of student nurses, brave young women who were killed by bombs during the Second World War. Okinawans had suffered at the hands of both the Japanese and the Americans, and these young women had been killed while trying to succour the wounded, on this last stepping stone of the Pacific War.

I was moved to see throngs of schoolchildren in the museum, gazing solemnly at the photographs of girls their own age, while a delicate music played behind. I wrote this piece on the spot, a tribute to the valour and compassion of the young nurses.

Death of Maidens

From the mouth of the cave
to the hollowed chamber underneath
is a journey we have made
in a few minutes, but for the maidens
it was darkness; a choking, burning grave,

From which their faces now rise,
young, still smiling, strong,
to the strains of sad, sweet music.
Black-uniformed schoolgirls throng
around what might be their own photographs,
all that withstood the 'typhoon of steel and bombs.'

You must remember us.
We will remember them.
It must never happen again,
on this elongated, serrated,
almost happy Okinawa island.

Paul Muldoon

This poem, a translation of 'An Lon Dubh Báite' by
Séamas Dall Mac Cuarta, is about suppression in the
aftermath of the defeats at Aughrim and the Boyne, and
the Penal Laws, when native Irish culture was all but
rubbed out.

The Drowned Blackbird

O beautiful daughter of Conn O'Neill,
you've slept long after your great loss.
Don't let your noble kinsmen hear you wail
for your one precious thing amid all the dross.

The music of that lively, lightsome bird
has gone from you, my bright seagull, all gone.
But there's a silver lining to every cloud.
Leave off your handclaps and ullagones.

From your handclaps and howls
of grief, hold off, my little chickabiddy;
O beautiful daughter of Conn O'Neill,
on a common bird don't waste your pity.

My pretty one that sprang from Ulster's high kings,
compose yourself, lest you go out of your mind
for the sake of a bird, albeit the sweetest that sings.
It's washed white now, see, in a bucket of lime.

An Lon Dubh Báite

A iníon álainn Choinn Uí Néill,
is fada do chuan tar éis d'áir;
is nach gcluin uaisle do chine féin
tú ag caoineadh do spré tar éis a bháis.

Ceiliúr an éin lúfair luaith,
theastaigh uait, a fhaoileann bhán;
cha bhíonn tubaiste ach mar mbíonn spré,
is déansa foighid ó ghreadadh lámh.

Ó ghreadadh lámh is ó shileadh rosc,
glacsa tost, a fhaoileann úr;
a iníon álainn Choinn Uí Néill,
fá bhás an éin ná fliuch do shúil.

A fhaoileann a d'fhás ó ardrí Uladh na rí,
fuirigh mar tá, is fearr é nó imeacht le baois;
fá d'éan beag a b'áille gáire ar imeall na gcraobh,
chan ceist duit a bhás go brách is é nite le haol.

                    Séamas Dall Mac Cuarta (1647-1733)

Richard Murphy

Prison

Losing your pen in the body-search behind
My dustbin-columned classical façade,
You're led by intercrural routes to find
Your gypsy friend, trussed in my fixed abode.

Before he lost his capricious boyhood, grew
A centaur's beard, hooves, haunches in relief,
Did you cage him with hubristic love? You knew
His touching thievery often gave you life.

Free to face across doubly screened zoo wire,
Stop-watched by warders in a cell, you meet,
Deterred by a faecal smell, beyond desire
Where words fail to regenerate, but cheat.

Poor old people he robbed in bed at night.
What sentence did your teaching help him write?

Eiléan Ní Chuilleanáin

I wrote this poem at the time when a number of women who had lived and died in a Magdalene asylum were reburied in Glasnevin cemetery without the knowledge of their relatives, because the site of the asylum had been sold. It is not intended as an attack on the nuns who gave them refuge but it is a poem on the right to a name, to recognition and to a record of one's life. It is also a plea to the injured for forgiveness.

Translation

for the reburial of the Magdalenes

The soil fraying and sifting evens the score –
There are women here from every county
Just as there were in the laundry,

Where white light blinded and bleached out
The high relief of a glance, where steam danced
Around stone drains and giggled and slipped across
    water.

Assist them now, ridges under the veil, shifting
Searching for their parents, their names,
The edges of words grinding against nature,

As if, when water sank between the rotten teeth
Of soap, and every grasp seemed melted, one voice
Had begun, rising above the shuffle and hum

Until every pocket in her skull blared with the note –
Allow us to hear it now, sharp as an infant's cry
While the grass thrives like steam rising –

Washed clean of idiom : the baked crust
Of words that made my temporary name
A parasite that grew in me : that spell
Lifted : I lie in earth sifted to dust :
Clattering keys I bore slacken and fall :
I rise and forget : a cloud over my time.

Nuala Ní Dhomhnaill

Dubh

(Ar thitim Srebrenica, 11ú Iúil, 1995)

Is lá dubh é seo.
Tá an spéir dubh.
Tá an fharraige dubh.
Tá na gáirdíní dubh.

Tá na crainn dubh.
Tá na cnoic dubh.
Tá na busanna dubh.
Tá na carranna a thugann na páistí ar scoil ar maidin
   dubh.

Tá na siopaí dubh.
Tá a bhfuinneoga dubh.
Tá na sráideanna dubh (is ní le daoine é).
Tá na nuachtáin a dhíolann an cailín dubh go bhfuil an
   folt láidir dubh uirthi
dubh dubh dubh.

Tá an damh dubh.
Tá an gadhar dubh.
Tá capall úd Uíbh Ráthaigh dubh.
Tá gach corr-éan a scinneann amach as an ealta dubh.
An chaoire dhubh a sheasann amach de ghnáth i lár an
   tréada,
ní heisceacht í níos mó mar tá na caoirigh ar fad dubh.

Tá na prátaí dubh.
Tá na turnapaí dubh.
Tá gach bileog cabáiste a chuirfeá síos i dtóin corcáin
   dubh.

Tá an sáspan dubh.
Tá an ciotal dubh.
Tá gach tóin corcáin as seo go Poll Tí Liabáin dubh.

Tá na Caitlicigh dubh.
Tá na Protastúnaigh dubh.
Tá na Seirbigh is na Cróátaigh dubh.
Tá gach uile chine a shiúlann ar dhromchla na cruinne
an mhaidin dhubh seo samhraidh dubh.

Tá na polaiticeoirí ar sciobaidh
is iad ag baint na gcos is na n-eireaball dá chéile
ag iarraidh a chur ina luí orainn
nach fada go mbeidh gach dubh ina gheal.

Is an té a leomhadh a mhisneach dó
nó a chreidfeadh an méid a deireann siad
níor mhiste dó b'fhéidir an cheist a chur
ab ann ab amhlaidh a chiallaíonn sé seo anois
nach mbeidh ins gach dubhthréimhse ach seal?

Ach ní dhéanfadsa.
Mar táimse dubh.
Tá mo chroí dubh
is m'intinn dubh.
Tá m'amharc ar feadh raon mo radhairce dubh.
Tá an dubh istigh is amuigh agam díbh.

Mar gach píosa guail nó sméar nó airne,
gach deamhan nó diabhal nó daradaol,
gach cleite fiaigh mhara nó íochtar bhonn bróige,
gach uaimh nó cabha nó poll tóine
gach duibheagán doimhin a shlogann ár ndóchas
táim dubh dubh dubh.
Mar tá Srebrenica, cathair an airgid,
'Argentaria' na Laidne,
bán.

Black

(Translated by Paul Muldoon)
On the Fall of Srebrenica, July 11th 1995

A black day, this.
The sky is black.
The sea is black.
The gardens are black.

The trees are black.
The hills are black.
The buses are black.
The cars bringing the kids to school are black.

The shops are black.
Their windows are black.
The streets are black (and I don't mean with people).
The newspapers sold by the dark girl with the great
    head of dark hair
are black, black, black.

The ox is black.
The hound is black.
The very horse from Iveragh is black.
The bird suddenly out of sync with the flock is black.
The black sheep that stood out from the ordinary run of
    sheep no longer stands out, for all the sheep are black.

The spuds are black.
The turnips are black.
Every last leaf of cabbage in the pot is black.

The saucepan is black.
The kettle is black.

The bottom of every pot from here to the crack of
    doom is black.

The Catholics are black.
The Protestants are black.
The Serbs and Croatians are black.
Every tribe on the face of the earth this blackest of
    black mornings black.

The politicians are scuffling about
biting the legs and tails off each other
trying to persuade us
to look on the bright side.

Anyone who might be inclined
to take them at their word
would do well, maybe, to ask
why they think it goes without saying
that every black cloud has a silver lining.

I myself won't be the one.
For I'm black.
My heart is black and my mind is black.
Everything that falls into my field of vision is black.
I'm full of black rage.
There's a black mark against all your names.

Like each and every lump of coal, every blackberry and sloe
and demon and devil and Devil's Coachman,
every grave and cave and arsehole,
every bottomless pit in which we lose all hope,
I'm black as black can be.

Now that Srebrenica, that silver city –
'Argentaria', as the Romans called it –
is suddenly blank.

Mary O'Donnell

This poem was in part influenced by my reading Martin Gilbert's war history, simply called *Holocaust*. In a way the book contained nothing I didn't more or less know already, yet the interminable cataloguing of atrocities left me unable to quite finish the book. The events at Babi Yar, however, never left my head. Babi Yar epitomises the system which characterises all genocides. That system is no different in some respects from contemporary atrocities, the torchings, rapings, mutilations, the deliberate humiliation and denigration of certain races of people. I'm thinking of the Marsh Arabs, for example, of the Kurds, of the people of southern Sudan. Those are just a few. In fact, there are hundreds of examples of interracial and genocidal hatred throughout the planet today, all simmering away, festering, limiting the potential of economically poor men and ensuring that the women in particular often remain largely illiterate and responsible for too much of the physical work of subsistence as well as for bearing children. As for the children? Sickness, early mortality, stunted physical and intellectual growth are the legacy. This legacy is accepted by most of us, simply by being passive.

Lament for Babi Yar

Babi Yar is a ravine outside Kiev where 30,000 Jewish men, women and children were shot in September 1941 within a space of three days by the Einsatzgruppe during the German offensive on Russia.

This grave will not settle:
Ash-grey soil still shifts and sighs,

Bones protrude to question trees
That stood by as they fell.

No silence either at Kiev, Lvov,
Where synagogues torched

With the skin of local Jewry.
That much is the same.

Voices from Vietnam, Africa, Tehran,
Beirut, Sao Paolo, Sudan,

Still scream for food and mercy,
Legs broken, heads smashed

By rite of hand, machete and gunbutt.
No time to wonder about God's hand

Outstretched to the just,
The force of will that rolls

Like slow poison across mountains,
Down rivers, in valleys of dreams.

The children are dying, even yet,
Tumble into the waiting pits,

Unavenged by angels
With warm wings to raise; even yet

When babies are split on stone,
Solicitude hovers like a cotton bomb

In circles where tea is sipped –
Homage paid to safety and rightness,

The relief of death from a distance.
But the grave will not settle:

Sobs thicken among the trees,
Crackle on the frost at Babi Yar.

I fume at this aloneness:
Though redemption shine on every dawn,

We dare not forgive ourselves.

Bernard O'Donoghue

I have chosen this poem because it was written in the late 1980s when the unenlightened British Government of the time was trying to bring in the infamous 'clause 28' intended to reduce the supposed influence of gay teachers in schools. To the credit of the British people, it got short shrift and was dropped. But it brought to mind a number of late eighteenth-century Irish pronouncements, such as the great epigram by John Philpot Curran which appears at the head of the poem. Vigilance *is* needed, to be on guard against erosions of liberty which may prove to be the thin end of an autocratic wedge.

Fuente Vaqueros, mentioned in the poem, was the home town of the Spanish poet-playwright Lorca who was killed during the Spanish Civil War because he was gay. And the particular occasion of the poem was an excellent television programme (made by an ex-student of mine, George Case) called 'The Forgotten Holocaust', about the treatment of gypsies throughout Europe in the course of World War II. They were wiped out in huge numbers but nobody knows *what* numbers because they lack any organized writing or commemorative system. So the poem raises the question of the treatment of travellers in Ireland and the grudging tolerance of 'temporary dwellings prohibited'.

The State of the Nation

'The condition upon which God hath given liberty to man is eternal vigilance'
(John Philpot Curran, 1790)

Before I fell asleep, I had been reading
How in the Concentration Camps, alongside
The Jewish personal effects, were stored
For future reference gypsies' earrings,
Scarves and the crystal globes in which they saw

The future; and how the new authorities
Swept through Fuente Vaqueros, smashing guitars.

The book was open still when I woke up
At dawn and, not reassured by the May chorus
From the cypresses, ran to the encampment
At the crossroads where the slow smoke curled by the
    sign
'Temporary Dwellings Prohibited'.
Still there; spread in dew along the hedges
Were gossamer and shawls and tea-towels.

A chained dog watched me peering under
The first canvas flap. Empty. The rest the same.
Not a soul in any tent. I straightened up
And listened through the sounds of morning
For voices raised in family rows, or their ponies
Tocking back from venial raids, bringing home
Hay, a clutch of eggs, unminded pullets.

Dennis O'Driscoll

1989 was the best of years. It was the worst of years. It was the year of Wenceslas Square and the year of Tiananmen Square. My poem '1989' ends, however, on Liberty Square in Thurles, County Tipperary – a long way from Peking and from Prague. My younger brother, Declan and his friends had been ticked off by a Garda for talking at a corner of the square after midnight. They had come, not from the Chinese take-away, but from an Amnesty International meeting.

1989

Peking students on their black bikes;
shoals wavering through river-wide squares,
merging and separating in the sun,
fish that test the purity of a habitat . . .

They remind me of school-going cyclists
in my childhood, chains clenching teeth
for the final assault on Liberty Square.
(That was Thurles in the late sixties,
Mao's book colouring the thoughts
of a few red-headed pupils.)

Tiananmen Square was cleared by guns.
On Wenceslas Square, the crowds cheered
as the guard changed, bringing relief
to banned philosophers, night-watchmen,
who had waited for the light to dawn.

All was quiet on Liberty Square
in this year of revolutions,
just some lads in drunken dispute
tripping from the Chinese take-away
or my young brother and his friends
urged by a policeman to move on,
not to disturb the peace
of sleepy residents
with talk of world events.

Desmond O'Grady

This poem derives from the dynastic and the folkloric literature of Egypt 4500 years ago. Today we are as guilty of mass murder by bomb and embargo and of adult and child abuse as was the case then. Every sane human has the universal right to live life as one chooses if it does not prevent others living theirs as they choose.

In the House of Commons

Based on the Egyptian Fourth Dynasty (c. 2575–c. 2465 BC) prophecy of Nefer-rohu

He brooded over what's happened
He said:

'Silence can only mean repression.
There's wild terror abroad
and the great man is a thing
of the past in our time.

Quit all laxity,
it daily stares from every face.
Rise up against what confronts you,
for what's been done
is what's not done.

This land is so completely destroyed
that nothing remains; that not so much
as the black under a nail survives
what was fated.

There's been such destruction
there's no one left who's concerned;
no one who speaks, no one who weeps.

When clouds cover the sun,
then everyone stands blind
for lack of it
and nothing survives.

I speak what's before my face:
The river runs dry. Sailors
want water to sail their ships on.
The river's course has become a sandbank
and the sandbank's piled high against the flood.
Everything good's gone and the land lies prostrate.
Enemies rise in the east and in the west.
And men enter their fortresses. The beasts
of the wild descend to the very doors without fear,
for want of someone to hunt them away.
The land runs riot and no one
forsees the outcome – hidden from speech and
sight and hearing. Faces gape deaf, confronted
with silence. Men take up weapons of war,
beg for the bread of blood and laugh
with the hysterical laughter of sickness.
I see no one to weep for a death
and man's heart, separated completely
from mourning, seeks selfishly only for self.
People turn their backs while one man
murders another. Sons slaughter their fathers,
brothers each other. Mouths choke with the cry
of "love me!" Man holds man in hate
to silence what mouth may speak.
If any man answers, arms rise up with sticks
and shouts of "Kill him! Kill him!"
Nobody knows when midday falls, for the sun
casts no shadow. I show you a land
in confusion, with mankind living in graveyards.
You must begin the foundations
of your world all over again.'

Sheila O'Hagan

Antigone is the universal heroine of compassion and heroism. I have always admired her for her staunch conviction that she had the right to bury her brother, Polynices, whatever his crime. Through her defiance she faced death at the hands of Creon, the king, who had her walled up in a cave. He later relented and came to release her but she was already dead.

She stands for the fortitude of women in the terrible ravages of war, and she is the heroine of Sophocles' drama *Antigone* and of Euripides' *Phoenissae*.

Antigone

There is no light. She breathes slowly,
Allows herself an hour for dreaming –
Of spring in Thebes, wildflowers barbarous
On the hills, air tumbling between
Her thighs her arms her smallest bones.
By starlight, she had crept from Argos
To track her bad boy brother, used
Hands and nails to claw earth for his grave,
Knew that like the last bright star
She would disappear before morning.

Walled in stone, her time has come.
She spits the dark out of her mouth
And with a cry of the thing done
Defiance becomes myth, her soul
Fills the space of that sentinel star
To lamplight all the nights when a sister
Creeps out along the pitted road
To lay a coat on the riven body of her brother.

Mary O'Malley

I am honoured to contribute in some small way to work I consider perhaps the most important on the planet. This poem is of course dedicated to that unknown child, to every unknown child. But it also relates to that single moment of imagination and courage in our recent history, Mary Robinson's visit to Somalia. For all our charity, I am not proud of Ireland's political action on human rights.

I am sending you this poem because it is sometimes the business of an artist to look into the eyes of a child that the world has abandoned. The eyes of the child in this photograph have never left me from the moment I saw them in a bookshop four years ago. The face of the child has been between me and every poem I have written since. It is the face of the human being in Marina Tsvetayeva's 'Art in the Light of Conscience' when she writes: 'To be a human being is more important because it is more needed . . . ' She was writing at a time in Russian history when artists were the voices of the country and the keepers of its values.

Given that this is a country that prides itself on giving as charity, is it not time to change our attitudes to the people those black babies might become, to the nature of the Gorta box, to the immediate plight of children abandoned on our own streets?

I question the safe distance of the artist in today's Ireland, and of those who affect a tired stance of indifference which says that to write of the plights of others, of abuses of human rights, is to abuse them in some way. Such a negation of the true nature of art appals me, as much on account of its ignorance as its lack of conscience. I am sending this particular poem because, in this time of greed and plenty, the eyes of the children accuse us all and because the face in the photograph is that of my child, and yours.

The Abandoned Child

For Mary Robinson
After a photograph by Don McClellan

This is a simple photograph, a black and white picture
of a child lying in the dust. She has no name.
Call her Baby, Beauty, Unbeloved, she is the face of
  our time.

She is thrown on the earth afraid, abandoned at the
  limit
of word and note and brushstroke.
Every poem pauses here. Important questions are
  decided:

Who will feed the child, the price of corn, what
  happens
to the planets when they die; and how long
do the doomed beauties last with the cameras gone.

The theory holds that a shrunken star will collapse
into a ball so tight, not even light will escape.
Into this invisible hole anything may fall, and has.

As to the children, the books are silent or advise
metaphorical distance. Only the songs remember
the unbreachable chasm between jazz notes,

where dead loves hang. She would be twenty,
maybe twenty-five now, a wife, a washerwoman, a
  physicist
spreading chaos across the stars. In her alternative
  Universe

there would be dishes to be washed, children to be
sent to school and minded. She might even now
be writing up a formula on her IBM compatible,

a theorem to predict the trajectory of a mother's kiss
But in the known world money changed hands. Prisons
    filled
and the crowd stampeded. She is most likely dead.

She has no name, this beauty lying in the dirt
between well made sonnets and free verse,
without an I or you or us, between the hand's release

and the rattle of the Gorta box. Read her eyes.
The Universe is made up in equal measure of tears
and hunger and bits of string, the old dimensions

and her face has more agony than a medieval Christ.
Her poem is the soundless howl of light streaming
into the black hole of heaven. Trying eternally to get
    out.

Cathal Ó Searcaigh

Isaac Rosenberg was an English poet-soldier killed in the First World War.

Do Isaac Rosenberg

Le bánú an lae agus muid ag teacht ar ais
i ndiaidh a bheith ag suirí i mbéal an uaignis
d'éirigh na fuiseoga as poill agus prochóga Phrochlais

agus chuimhnigh mé ortsa, a Isaac Rosenberg,
cathshuaite i dtailte treascartha na Fraince, ag éisteacht
le ceol sítheach na bhfuiseog le teacht an lae

agus tú ag pilleadh ar do champa, thar chnámha
    créachta
do chairde, ruaithne reatha na bpléascán, creathánach,
ag deargadh an dorchadais ar pháirc an chatha.

Ag éisteacht le meidhir na bhfuiseog idir aer agus uisce
thaibhsigh do dhánta chugam thar thalamh eadrána na
    síoraíochta, líne,
ar líne, stadach, scáfar mar shaighdiúirí ó bhéal an áir

agus bhain siad an gus asam lena gcuntas ar an Uafás:
as duibheagán dubh na dtrinsí, as dóchas daortha na
    n-óg, as ár
agus anbhás, d'éirigh siad chugam as corrabhuais
    coinsiasa –

mise nach raibh ariamh sa bhearna bhaoil, nach dtug
ruathar mharfach thar an mhullach isteach sa chreach,
nár fhulaing i dtreascairt dhian na fola;

nach bhfaca saighdiúirí óga mar bheadh sopóga ann,
    caite
i gcuibhrinn mhéith an áir, boladh bréan an bháis
ag éirí ina phláigh ó bhláth feoite a n-óige;

nach raibh ar maos i nglár is i gclábar bhlár an chatha,
nár chaill mo mheabhair i bpléasc, nár mhothaigh an
    piléar
mar bheach thapaidh the ag diúl mhil fhiáin m'óige.

Ó ná hagair orm é, a Isaac Rosenberg, d'ainm a lua,
mise atá díonaithe i mo dhánta i ndún seo na Seirce
agus creach dhearg an chogaidh i gcroí na hEorpa go
    fóill.

Ach bhí mo chroí lasta le lúcháir agus caomhchruth
    álainn
mo leannán le mo thaobh, gach géag, gach alt, gach
    rinn,
gach ball de na ballaibh ó mhullach go talamh mo
    mhealladh,

sa chruth go gcreidim agus muid i mbachlainn a chéile
go bhfuil díon againn ar bhaol, go bhfuil an saol lán
    d'fhéile,
go bhfuil amhrán ár ngrá ina gheas ar gach aighneas.

Agus tá na fuiseoga ag rá an rud céanna liomsa a dúirt
    siad leatsa
sular cuireadh san aer tú, sular réabadh do chnámha –
Is fearr cumann agus ceol ná cogadh agus creach;

agus cé nach raibh mé ariamh i mbéal an chatha
agus cé nach bhfuil caite agam ach saol beag suarach,
    sabháilte,
ag daingniú mo choirnéil féin agus ag cúlú ó
    chúiseanna reatha;

ba mhaith liom a dhearbhú duitse, a fhile, a d'fhán go
   diongbháilte
i mbun d'fhocail, a labhair le lomchnámh na fírinne ó
   ár an chatha –
go bhfuil mise fosta ar thaobh an tSolais, fosta ar
   thaobh na Beatha.

For Isaac Rosenberg

Translated by Frank Sewell

At dawn, we gave up our courting
out in the wilderness. Larks soared
from the bog-holes and hollows of Prochlais.

Then I thought of you, Isaac Rosenberg,
war-weary in the 'torn fields of France',
stunned by the siren larks, one dawn

as you returned to your camp over the ruined
bones of friends, shaken, with bombs
pouncing on the red and black battlefield.

The larks' joy between air and water
brought your poems across eternity's barricade, line
by line, stutteringly, scared, like soldiers in battle,

and they stopped me in my tracks with horror:
the dark pits of trenches, youth's smashed-up
hopes, the carnage wracked my conscience,

I who was never within an ounce of my life,
who never had to pile over the top and into battle,
who never lost out in any of the bloodshed,

I who never saw young soldiers torched
and dumped in an open field of slaughter,
their blighted bodies stinking with death,

I who was never plunged in the mud and mire,
never shell-shocked or stung by a bullet
sucking out my life like some crazy bee honey . . .

O, don't mind me, Isaac Rosenberg, calling you
from here, my safe-house of love poems,
while Europe still eats its heart out;

only mine was light with joy, my lover
beside me in all his glory, every limb,
joint, rim, every bit of him tempting me

to believe that we're safe together,
that life is for feasting
and love wards off trouble.

The larks tell me what they told you,
before you were blown to pieces –
that love and music beat war and empire;

and though I've never been in action,
though I've had a safe, ordinary life,
looking after my own and keeping out of it,

I want to assure you, poet whose truth
was bared to the bones in World War 1,
I too am on the side of the light, and of life.

Micheal O'Siadhail

I have chosen this poem because the diary of the Dutch-
woman Etty Hillesum on which this poem is based has
always struck me as one of the most powerful and inspiring
testaments that I know of to human growth and maturity
in the face of suffering. I think it is the gentle, at first even
confused, courage and ordinariness of her witness that I
love. But above all it's her joyful determination to give her
own life in service that seems particularly appropriate to
Amnesty celebration.

from *Etty Hillesum*

And now I'm alone and here for everyone.
To bear all, growing stronger in the bearing.
Where I'm cut short, someone will carry on.

Joy. Memories of jasmine. My blistered feet.
Pogroms. Unspeakable horrors. All one whole.
To live long enough to fathom a little of it.

The dumpy woman with such greasy black hair
I imagine behind a washtub on Jodenbreestraat.
A hunchbacked Russian with that big-eyed stare.

All those worries about clothing, about food.
I want my life to turn into one great prayer.
So happen what may, it's bound to be good.

Is life glorious and magnificent? This desire
That we build some day a whole new world
A spring in my step as I walk by the barbed wire.

Are we given more to bear than we can shoulder?
And beyond that will we break? Some younger
Ones seemed shattered in spirit; those older

Take root in this wasteland soil. An eyesore.
A few lupins and seagulls. But my father smiles:
Jews in a desert? We've seen the landscape before.

Waxen faces. Registrations. Friskings. Process.
Roughly seventy people to a sealed goods wagon.
Bucket in middle; for the sick a paper mattress.

A fine-grained message as wagon No. 12 careers
Towards Poland. Some farmer stoops to pick up
Her final postcard from those crammed years.

The web-spinning spider lets its thread unwind,
Then, follows on. A life stretching beyond itself.
We were singing as we left the transit camp behind.

Michael O'Sullivan

I have chosen this poem because I believe the artist has the responsibility to confront the darkest areas of experience, however unpopular that might be. In poetry, as in life, nothing changes without courageous leaps into the unknown; without danger there is no true progress. True poems are fantastically difficult and complex, however effortless they might seem. I trust this poem because it continues to clear rooms, both at readings and in my own mind. Yet, beneath the surface violence of the poem lies a bedrock of redemption and love.

And After This Our Exile

Do the halfdead know what life
his loins will give?

Naked and erect
in passionate moonlight
he scrutinises each plot
like a map
with millionsided destinations
culminating in the fury of going.

Everywhere the earth stirs –
the moon subscribes to shallow burials.

Gripped by frost
grass crackles underfoot.

He targets recent graves,
watches earthdulled hair flourish
with shards of bone & fingernail
just above the surface.

Limbs already respond
to his crazed stealth,
plants quickly germinating
in matrices of bood.

Blind tendrils grope for him:
the limbs of those imperfectly killed
by weak violence
& left in festering state
to wait in clay
for a Resurrection
which loses impetus halfway to heaven.

Surrounding vegetation too discovers
its new sex
in reprogrammed cells,
each one a sacrifice to generation.

They guide him,
eunuchs suddenly potent in a brothel.

Untutored loins engage some twisting skulls.
Curved bone vibrates and swells.
Membranes revive
fleshed by the aroma of his skin.
He straddles each grave once,
leaving a measured pearl,
the scent from which will spread
in maddened whirls.

Rapidly he leaps to the next plot,
expertly depositing each opal drop
with insectine precision.

Soil patches groan.
Tombstones topple
from torsos breaking through
the evenness of slabs.
In gathering crescendo timbers split:
he's harnessed strength all the living dead possess,
harvesting their musclebloom
before the moon goes down.

Limbs race to silver air
faster than his own seed
shooting to the soil.

Nearby evergreen trees are withering:
tenacious wax moonwrenched,
dripping with white acids
in imitation of him.

Each leaf surrenders life
to the convulsion. He gauges
each stalactite in night's cave
with compound eye.

He squats and waits
for other limbs to break swaying sod.

Soon a hand probes through.
He pulls the arm,
but tendons dully snap.
So he clears the earth around,
consummate white nurse
of the nerve earth bed.

He tongues quivering flesh
each lick restoring lustre to the limbs,
each grasp glow to her muscles.

Life cascades through her –
her stifled laugh is everywoman's,
its thrill sustained by fire
forbidden in the world.

He smiles,
feeling on her stomach
a dream incarnate.

She's sweeter now than rotting forest,
delerious with rose and fermentation,
far sweeter than if she'd danced
newbathed to nectar sheets.

She whines her soul though pus
as he sucks the ruby mass,
a doctor extracting poison from a wound.

No camera could catch the exquisite bite –
speed and bliss combine, accelerate
beyond that point where impetus consumes
all trace of vagrant matter.

Tenderly he breaks each bone.
Swaying she moans in rhythm.
She takes her marrow in her palm
enveloping his penis. The lubricant compels
sharp stars to coalesce.
She presses flaked bloodflow
between his buttocks,
her earwax stings his eyes.
Chewing her liver
he finds more eloquent tongue.

They heave to her beginning
while he gives her small hands strength
to crush her own skull.
Both watch in awe
grey matter mixed with seed,
blood with pulsating earth.

Her wombcells wildly multiply
& just as quickly burn
scorched by his clamorous seed.
She writhes, bones freely breaking.
She chants 'feet', 'mystery' & 'line'
enveloping them both
in a choral cup.

Her face cuts through his spine.
Its flesh carves down his legs.
She clasps his bodysoul,
he crushes her pelvis
his penis still shuddering
in a sucking cave.
Her vocal chords explode.
They clamp in harmony.
She leaks into his bone
pregnant with velvet death.
Their mixing blood congeals.
He dies
choking on a rich chunk of her womb.

On their entagled ribs
bright flakes of morning snow.

Tom Paulin

The analogies between Palestinian and Irish history, between Jewish and Irish history are well known. I chose this poem because I deplore the treatment of the Palestinian people by the Israeli state.

Palestinian Free State

One by one and two by two
they're blowing up the Arab houses
– houses? Arabs?
only shadows live here
and all that shadows need
in Eretz Israel
is one bright wall
to fall against

in the crystal dazzle
called Tel Aviv
there appears a city
of tight holiday homes
where all the settlers dress
in new store clothes
to praise the Leica's
optical hygiene
– what you see is what you see
soon that little puddle
of shadow history
will be a pocked dryness
and a wisp of steam

Justin Quinn

Manumission

Recently illiteracy, murder and malnourishment
were re-invented; the logo designed so that

these new products will leap out
from the shelves when you wheel down past

to get your week's stuff – books, food, things
to wipe the baby's ass and your own; designed it

so that when you lift your hand out through the space,
the very air, of the supermarket that's faceted with
    choice

you'll feel that this product is for you,
that your personality is best expressed

though its purchase; it's *you*; you know it too
and ferry it home with the kind of consumer pride

you associate with the 1940s and '50s
when the world was a better place, and Ma

was not your Da in drag (like now)
and men in suits met in high-ceilinged rooms to

say that there are rights, that there are
human rights, and you could look out the

window into the suburban haze and not feel
that any moment your own hands

would swoop down from the skies
with exceptionally intricate weaponry destroying

foliage, cats, schoolchildren, you also,
while voiceovers promise plenitude, the trickle-down

effect, World-Bank suits arriving any minute now, they
    say;
a time when your hand moving through

the air, whatever air that be,
was not what it (lift it up and look) is today.

Maurice Scully

Steps

a

driving in a red dustcloud
for hours years wandering
wondering how to

connect

this stone to that hut with
precision tact two hands one
gift wait listen right
left shimmering elastic

wallhome
(not any other barrier
but a breeze over it)
welcoming. conduit.

b

blue flower strong stem
oval stone in the stream

I was stepping lightly home
(the baby developing)

starlings' jabber-click
cutting with the burin nick

conical hills stone outcrop
two swans one rooftop

dead flower dead stem
dead stone in the stream

a fish shadows by. a cloud.
a bird. wake up, coward.

c

window lit
fire in the grate
door closed over
table set

the food being ready
ready the appetite
(in dreams begin steadi-
ness) come, sit −

peeling a piece
of bark to get
the smell of
the tree feeding −

when threads mesh as they cross
over they sing to us.

this is how to live.

Peter Sirr

This poem is in three sections; they're really quite distinct parts, written at different times and each responding to a different aspect of the way in which people kill each other in judicial or quasi-judicial fashion. The first part refers to the gruesome custom in Dublin's Newgate Prison of bringing the coffin to the cell of a condemned prisoner well in advance of the execution, as a kind of grim reminder of his impending death. What I was really interested in here was the kind of mind that devises these kinds of torments: the idea that someone sits down and thinks these things through, making notes, refinements, applying his full ingenuity to the task.

The second part was written after reading an account by Robert Fisk of the massacres by Croats of Serbs during the Second World War, and of the crimes committed by various camp-guards and executioners. The article was accompanied by photographs, one of which showed the young executioner pausing in mid-murder to smile at the camera. As always in these cases, it's the matter-of-fact, banal attitude of the killers that appals as much as the deed. You know, given a chance, that they would do it again and think nothing of it.

The final section was written after reading a book called *Dublin Hanged*, an account of capital punishment in Dublin in the eighteenth century, and also coming across an article describing a cache of bones of apparently executed people found near Christchurch in the process of building excavations. It's hard, now, to imagine the central role of public executions in Dublin street life for much of its history, and the outrage of the populace when, for a time, hangings were confined within the prison. They wanted their death-theatre and were not going to be done out of it. The poem's partly about that, about the fact that lots of people actively enjoy executions, out of sadism, *schadenfreude*, or moral righteousness, and partly about how difficult it is to respond meaningfully to the daily onslaught of murder or tragic death, how sympathy and outrage are always nudged by indifference, by the usual pressures of a life. You can watch the bloodiest slaughter on the news and still stay tuned for the film or the sitcom, the current of concern ebbing away until it disappears completely, to be reawakened by the next newsflash . . .

The Universal Remote

The hangman brought the coffin
two days ago, it is the tradition
it is an idea
arrived at one night
after much thought, previous drafts
having failed to satisfy

brilliant dawning:
the death-table at which the victim
may entertain his final guests
enjoying a careless card-game
Concentration is difficult

but not impossible.
Then, too, the hangman's mask and the bowl
strapped to his back
deflecting fruit and stones
as he adjusts the rope, hempen

collar, ribald
and rapid succession of images
the hours nailed to a frame
of lovely syntax, the lines
rapt but unhurried, school
of exquisite detail

and unarguable closure

A hymn to the sagging crossbeam
on which hang is it thirteen?
Serbs 'like thrushes'

the decency of wood
to admit its weight:
any further you'd think

looking at the photograph
and the thing wouldn't be possible
but that would be pushing it

here also room to celebrate
the delicate features of
Nada Tanic-Luburic

and Maja Slomic-Buzdon
specialists in women prisoners
at Stara Gradiska

or the jaunty face of a young militiaman
eye on the camera, right hand
methodically sawing the neck

of Branko Jungic, villager. Later,
a cigarette in the head's mouth,
another picture.

On the shelf a stack of albums, an infinitum
of uniforms and shiny crests,
of smiles rising to dignity

from craft, to which they say Continue
we're still with you, sharp or blunt it's fun
but the trick with the light that will keep us strong

requires concentration

An evening auditioning the hanged
— noose of curiosity, rope of sympathy

the mind as ready, as remotely generous as for
the forest fire, the house fire, the plane nosing into the
    Pacific

as if to conjure a space important with their loss
their names in columns, lightly travelled

certain bodies borne off to the prosecutor's door
or dragged by Volunteers to the waiting professors

the urban renewal of the call
to have the deed brought back from behind the wall

where, for good order, they had placed it.
And it was granted, again

colourful scenes on the green, in the square
this on strangled and thrown upon the pyre

this one and his brother strung up yesterday
a harvest, recently, of botched bones

where the inexpertly hacked still lay
deep in the city . . . Gradually the crowd disperses, the
    vast square

turns to the narrowest alley
sweet with rage, grief, with the purest joy.

Eithne Strong

I submit this poem because it is witness to my firm belief
that change for the better in society begins with the self.
We, the people concerned about, engaged in, the struggle
for human rights, must first be aware of our inner selves,
must look to our personal orientations, values, integrity.
Systems are instruments of people: groupings of individuals.
The worth, the effectiveness of systems − organizations,
movements, governments − are to be measured by the
integrity of the individuals of which they are composed.

The symbol of Amnesty − the flame burning strongly
and through the constraints of imprisoning barbed wire −
I find sustaining, hopeful, signifying a persisting brightness
in the human spirit which encompasses mercy and forgiving-
ness. Ultimately, at the heart of things, it is in the personal
recognition and acknowledgement by each human being of
the rights of his fellow creature to fullest life, that
regeneration resides. I believe the poem 'Credo' reverberates
to the concepts of Amnesty.

Credo

I feel witness
to unchangingness
as well as change.

If I incline to
leave unmirrored
political moil, it is because

the human composition,
person to private person,
is my sphere, my particular

theme. In brief –
the things of state –
bland blue-suit smile,

smooth-shirt doubledo
(we beg true blue but
have them shot by dark);

lobbying;
feather-nesting; high inflate
of rigmarole; vigilant spite

that splits the nose
to spoil the party face –
all these things I have to see

as but reflections
in macro of doings round
the micro centre. As people

pattern in private
so, unchangingly, will they
projected in their public scale.

The central attitude
is inexorable: there is no
escape; life demands encounter

with figures like
fathers, brothers, lovers
rivals, mistresses, mothers, wives.

Inevitably national
and international are but larger
shapes of interpersonal procedures:

appetites and checks
that flux around the swallowing
demand of predatory devouring 'Me'.

Large happenings
in the state wear secondary
coverings. My bent is primary.

William Wall

When I was writing this poem I had in mind the way people can reject the existence of other people and other cultures, the way they can invalidate them. I wanted, firstly, to conjure a kind of culture and existence that was completely alien to us – the 'fire people'. But, as the poem says, 'this is not a curse or a visitation', and though we can reject that way of life, it could easily become our own, if we understood it.

The Fire People

'Not to release them from their ancient curse'
Derek Mahon 'Last of the Fire Kings'

Over there beyond that stretch of water
there are people who are born in fire:
their hair is the colour of fire
their eyes flash like lighthouses
their hands are as hot as steam
their loins are like cinders
their feet scorch the stones
their houses are built inside out
their roofs are open to the skies
& they sleep on water

& this is not a curse or a visitation
& they are not gods or devils
& they neither burrow nor fly.
It is just a different kind of life
& it would consume you entirely.

David Wheatley

This is a translation of Osip Mandelstam's 'Lines on the Unknown Soldier', one of the Russian poet's greatest meditations on suffering and violence.

Lines on the Unknown Soldier

after Mandelstam

1

Let this air stand by what we're told:
That his pounding heart so far away,
Even in the dugouts of this world,
Remains an ocean sightless to this day.

And stars—there must be more than twinkles in your
Eyes, seeing everything beneath
And knowing it's the judge and witness that were
Due cells blind as his till death.

How barren the seed would have to be to match
The rain, so evocative of his nameless manna,
Or how the wooden crosses stood watch
Over an ocean or a fallen banner!

And men will still go cold, fall sick, and worse,
Murder, shiver with the cold, and starve,
While the body of the unknown soldier's
Laid to rest in an infamous grave.

You, ailing swallow, I take for tutor –
Half-forgetting yourself how to fly –
How shall I steer round death without a rudder
Or, wingless, cheat the grave to mount on high?

And where Mikhail Lermontov's concerned,
Allow me to spell out for his benefit
How much the hunchback has to learn
From the death he sees reflected in the pit.

2
How these worlds menace
Us, like rustling grapes,
Hanging like stolen cities,
Golden slips of the tongue, calumnies –
Berries of the poisonous
Cold – marquees of tensile starscapes –
Stardust in golden, oily drops.

3
Signing the ether like a decimal point
The dazzle of speeds slowed down to a ray
Begins to trace a figure suffused with lucent
Pain and a mole of nullity.

Beyond the field of fields a new field
Is taking wing like a triangular crane –
The bright dust-road we see the news propelled
Along shines from battles long since done.

The news flies along a bright dust-road:
I am no Leipzig, no Waterloo,
No war of the tribes: I am fresh blood
But unspilt. It is from me that light will flow.

Deep inside the black marble oyster
Was where the flame of Austerlitz was extinguished.
The Mediterranean swallow's slit-eyes stare;
The trap is sprung in Egypt's plague-ridden waste.

4

The medley of an Arabian hodge-podge,
The dazzle of speeds slowed down to a ray –
And on its two splay feet the image
Falls athwart my eye.

The millions done to death on the cheap
Have trodden a path through the emptiness:
Good night to them, best wishes from the scarp
Of the earthen fortresses.

Trenched, incorruptible sky, sky of
Our almighty, wholesale morgue –
It is behind you, away from you, that I move
My lips, whole one, in the dark.

For the shell craters, embankments and screes
Over which he broods and frowns –
The pockmarked, sullen, powerless
Spirit of the overturned grave-stones.

5

How well the infantry dies
And how well the nightly choir sings
Over smiling flat-nosed Švejk,
The metatarsus, avian and chivalrous,
And Don Quixote's bird-lance.
The cripple befriends the man: there's work
Enough for both of them. The race
Of wooden crutches runs amok
Around the outskirts of the epoch.
Comradeship—ah, how the earth spins!

6

Must the whole skull be unpacked,
The brain-pan from temple to temple,
The dear eye-sockets be helpless
To resist the soldiers' onward trample?
The skull, unpacked of life all of a piece –
From temple to temple –
Teases itself with how well it was patched
Together, gleaming like a dome of tact
Frothing with thought to see its dreams reflect
Itself, the cup of cups, the lares and penates –
A mob-cap sewn like a starry scar –
The cap of joy–Shakespeare's father.

7

Ash-tree for clarity, sycamore for vigilance:
A homeward scramble tinged with scarlet
As though to swoon into speech with the heavens,
Both of them, in their colourless heat.

Only what's *passé* allies itself to us:
That isn't our downfall ahead, just one more error.
The struggle for the air I breathe – this
Glory I name beyond compare.

What good is the package of ready-made
Charm, stuck in a vacuum?
To send the scarlet-tinged white
Stars rushing back home?

And commending myself to my consciousness
With a half-fainting core
Of being I'll down this slop without choice –
Eat my head under fire!

Can you feel it, stepmother of the starlit
Bivouac, the night come down, the night ahead?

8
Aortas choke in blood. Row
Upon row you hear them whisper:
'I was born in ninety-four,'
'I was born two years before . . . '
And, holding on tight to
My worn-out birth-year
I whisper through bloodless lips: 'I saw
The light of day first two
Nights into the untrustworthy year
Of ninety-one. Now
The centuries encircle me with fire.'

Macdara Woods

The most immediate and elementary of all rights must be those of children, a home, education, nurturing. The right, in short, to be a child. This poem was written in 1993, in Italy, on the occasion of my son's setting out, in costume, to celebrate the carnevale of martedi grasso with his classmates, and is all that I, or any parent, can effectively hope to say in the end: go, with my blessing, know you will always be welcomed back and loved, and travel safely amid the dangers.

The distinguished songwriter/composer, Brendan Graham, adapted and put music on my poem for his song, 'Winter, Fire and Snow' to stunning effect and with great success. The song has been recorded a number of times on both sides of the Atlantic, by among others Nashville's Benita Hill, Eurovision winner Eimear Quinn, and initially by Riverdance's Katie McMahon and Anúna, who also performed it as part of the programme of the 1994 Amnesty Voices of the Disappeared Concert in the Gaiety Theatre, Dublin.

Fire and Snow and Carnevale

In winter fire is beautiful
beautiful like music
it lights the cave —
outside the people going home
drive slowly up the road — the strains
of phone-in Verdi on the radio
three hours back a fall of snow
sprinkled the furthest hill
where clouds have hung all winter

The day gets dark uneasy
dark and darker still
and you little son come home
riding the tail of the wind
in triumph – tall and almost ten
with confetti in your hair
home successful from the carnevale
with your two black swords
and your gold-handled knife

I feel the chill and hear
the absent sound of snow
when you come in –
white fantastic scorpions spit
in the fiery centre of the grate
plague pictures cauterised –
In winter fire is beautiful
and generous as music – may you
always come this safely home
in fire and snow and carnevale

Index of Titles

The Poets

Bardwell, Leland was born of Irish parentage in India in 1928 and returned to Ireland at an early age. A novelist and member of Aosdána, she is co-editor of *Cyphers* literary magazine. Her poetry collections include *The Mad Cyclist* (1970), *Dostoevsky's Grave: New and Selected Poems* (1991), *The White Beach* (1998) and *Pagan at the Table* (1998).

Berkeley, Sara was born in Dublin in 1967. She now lives in California. Her poetry collections are *Penn* (1986), *Home-Movie Nights* (1989), *New and Selected Poems* (1994) and *Facts About Water* (1995).

Boland, Eavan was born in Dublin in 1944. She is Melvin and Bill Lane Professor in the Humanities at Stanford University, California. Her recent poetry includes *In a Time of Violence (1994), Collected Poems (1995)* and *The Lost Land* (1998).

Bolger, Dermot was born in Dublin in 1959. The author of six novels (including *The Journey Home*, *A Second Life*, and *Father's Music*) and of seven plays (including *The Lament for Arthur Cleary* and *In High Germany*), he began as a poet and in 1998 published his first collection in a decade, *Taking My Letters Back*.

Boran, Pat was born in Portlaoise, County Laois in 1963. His poetry collections include *The Unwound Clock* (1990), *Familiar Things* (1993) and *The Shape of Water* (1996).

Brennan, Rory was born in Westport, County Mayo in 1945. His first poetry collection, *The Sea on Fire* (1978), won the Patrick Kavanagh Award. He has published two further collections, *The Walking Wounded* (1985) and *The Old in Rapallo* (1996).

Brett, Heather was born in Newfoundland in 1956, and grew up in County Antrim. Her first collection, *Abigail Brown* (1991), won the Brendan Behan Memorial Prize.

Bushe, Paddy was born in Dublin in 1948. He now lives in Kerry. His collections are *Poems With Amergin* (1989), *Teanga* (1990), *Counsellor* (1991) and *Digging Towards The Light* (1994).

Callaghan, Louise C. is a teacher in Dublin. Her poems have been widely published in magazines and journals in Ireland and abroad. She is currently completing her first collection, *The Palatine Daughter*.

Cannon, Moya was born in Dunfanaghy, County Donegal in 1956. She was awarded the 1991 Brendan Behan Memorial Award for her first collection, *Oar*. Her second collection is *The Parchment Boat* (1997).

Casey, Philip was born in London in 1951 and brought up in Gorey, County Wexford. His poetry collections include *After Thunder* (1985) and *The Year of the Knife: Poems 1980–1990* (1991). He is also a playwright and novelist.

Chapman, Patrick was born in 1968 and lives in Dublin. He is the author of three collections of poetry: *Jazztown* (1991), *The New Pornography* (1996) and *Proximity* (1999).

Clarkin, Sean was born in Wexford in 1941. A recipient of the Patrick Kavanagh Award, he has published one collection of poems, *Without Frenzy*.

Clifton, Harry was born in Dublin in 1952, has travelled widely and now divides his time between Paris and Dublin. *The Desert Route: Selected Poems 1973–88* was published in 1992, and a new collection, *Night Train through the Brenner* in 1994.

Coady, Michael was born in Carrick-on-Suir, County Tipperary in 1939. His collections include *Two for a Woman, Three for a Man* (1980), *Oven Lane* (1987) and *All Souls* (1998), an illustrated compendium of poetry and prose.

Collinge, Declan has published collections that include *Sealgaireacht* (1982), *Faoi Léigear* (1986) *Fearful Symmetry* (1990), *The Flowering Tree* (1991) and *A Page Falls Open* (1993).

Cowman, Roz was born in Cork in 1942. In 1985 she won the Patrick Kavanagh Award for poetry. A collection, *The Goose Herd,* was published in 1989.

Croft, David was born in Batley, West Yorkshire in 1964. His work has appeared in many books and periodicals. He has lived and worked in Dublin since 1992.

Cronin, Anthony was born in Wexford in 1928. He is a poet, critic and novelist, and the biographer of Flann O'Brien and Samuel Beckett.

Cullen, Leo was born in Templetouhy, County Tipperary and has lived in Dublin since 1967. His poetry and short fiction have appeared in several publications, and a prose work, *Clocking Ninety on the Road to Cloughjordan,* was published in 1994.

Curtis, Tony was born in Dublin in 1955. He is an award-winning poet and has published four collections, *Shifting of Stone* (1986), *Behind the Green Curtain* (1988), *This Far North* (1994) and *Three Songs of Home* (1998).

Daly, Padraig was born in Dungarvan, County Waterford in 1943 and is an Augustinian priest in Dublin. His collections include *Nowhere But in Praise* (1978), *This Day's Importance* (1981), *A Celibate Affair* (1984) and most recently *Out Of Silence* (1993).

Dawe, Gerald was born in Belfast in 1952. He has published four collections of poetry, most recently *Heart of Hearts*, as well as various works of criticism, and teaches at Trinity College Dublin. A new collection, *The Morning Train*, is due in 1999 along with his selected essays, *Stray Dogs and Dark Horses.*

Deane, Seamus was born in Derry in 1940. He has published several volumes of poetry, including *Selected Poems* (1988), a novel, *Reading in the Dark* (1996), which was shortlisted for the Booker Prize, and several volumes of critical essays.

de Fréine, Celia was born in Dublin and is a poet in Irish and English. Her work has been widely published. A bilingual collection, *Ar Mhuin an Albatrais/Ascending the Albatross* is forthcoming.

Delanty, Greg was born in Cork in 1958. His collections include *Cast in the Fire* (1986), *Southward* (1992), *American Wake* (1994) and *The Hellbox* (1998) and he has won many awards for his poetry.

de Paor, Louis was born in 1961. He has published several collections in Irish, most recently *Seo Siúd agus Uile* (Coiscéim, 1996) and bilingual collections, including *Gobán Cré is Cloch/Sentences of Earth and Stone* (1996).

Donovan, Katie was born in Dublin in 1962. Her poetry is collected in *Watermelon Man* (1993) and *Entering the Mare* (1997) and she has edited several anthologies.

Dorgan, Theo was born in Cork in 1953. His published works include *The Ordinary House of Love* (1991), *Rosa Mundi* (1995) and *Sappho's Daughter* (1998). He is Director of Poetry Ireland.

Duffy, Noel was born in Dublin in 1971. His poems have appeared in a number of poetry journals including *Poetry Ireland Review* and *Bellingham Review* (USA) and have been broadcast on radio.

Dunne, Oliver is a writer and collage-artist who lives and works in Dublin. His poems and short stories have appeared in various publications. He was shortlisted for The *Sunday Tribune*-Hennessy Literary award in 1995.

Durcan, Paul was born in Dublin in 1944. His collections include *The Berlin Wall Café* (1985), *Daddy, Daddy* (1990), winner of the Whitbread Poetry Prize, *Crazy about Women* (1995), *A Snail in My Prime* (1993), *Give Me Your Hand* (1994) and *Christmas Day* (1996).

Egan, Desmond was born in Athlone, County Westmeath in 1936. His poetry collections include *Midland* (1972), *Leaves* (1974), *Siege!* (1976), *Athlone?* (1980), *Seeing Double* (1983), *Collected Poems* (1983), *Poems for Peace* (1986), *A Song for My Father* (1989), *Selected*

Poems (1991) and *Peninsula* (1992).

Fallon, Peter was born in Germany in 1951. He is the founder and editor of Gallery Press. His own most recent volume, *News of the World: New and Selected Poems*, was published in 1998.

Fitzmaurice, Gabriel was born in Moyvane, County Kerry in 1952. He has published six collections of poetry in English, including *Rainsong* (1984) and *The Space Between: New and Selected Poems 1984–92* (1993), three collections in Irish and several collections of poetry in English and Irish for children.

Gorman, Michael was born in Sligo and lives in Barna, near Galway City. He is also an editor and playwright. A collection of poems, *Up She Flew*, was published in 1991.

Hardie, Kerry was born in 1951. She has won several awards for her poetry, including the *The Sunday Tribune*-Hennessy Literary Award in 1996. Her collection, *A Furious Place*, was published in 1996.

Hartnett, Michael was born in Croom, County Limerick in 1941. He is a poet in Irish and English and a translator. Collections in Irish include *Adharca Broic* (1978) and *An Lia Nocht* (1985). His most recent collection, *Selected and New Poems*, was published in 1994.

Haverty, Anne was born in County Tipperary. She is a biographer and has written a novel, *One Day as a Tiger* (1997). Her poetry has appeared in journals and magazines.

Healy, Dermot was born in Finea, County Westmeath in 1947. His works include a novel, *A Goat's Song* (1993), and a memoir, *The Bend for Home* (1996). His most recent poetry collection is *What the Hammer* (1998).

Heaney, Seamus was born in Mossbawn near Castledawson, County Derry in 1939. Since *Death of a Naturalist* in 1966, he has published nearly a score of books of poetry and associated work and was awarded the Nobel Prize for Literature in 1995. *The Spirit Level* (1996) is his most recent collection.

Higgins, Michael D. was born in Limerick in 1941 and has for many years been a public representative, holding a seat in Galway West for the Labour Party. He was Minister for Arts, Culture and the Gaeltacht from 1993–7. He has published two collections of poetry, *Betrayal* (1990) and *The Season of Fire* (1993). He was the first recipient of the Seán MacBride Peace Prize in 1992 and is a patron of Amnesty.

Johnston, Fred has published one novel and six volumes of poetry, the most recent of which is *True North* (1997). A short story collection, *Keeping the Night Watch*, was published in 1998.

Keane, Fergal was born in London in 1961 and reared in Dublin and Cork. He works as a special correspondent with the BBC and is the author of three non-fiction books, *Bondage of Fear*, *Season of Blood* and *Letter to Daniel*. He was recently awarded an OBE.

Le Marquand Hartigan, Anne was born in England. She has published four collections of poetry, including *Now is a Moveable Feast* and *Immortal Sins*. Her *Selected Poems* is due in 1999. She is also an artist and playwright.

Longley, Michael was born in Belfast in 1939. His published verse includes *No Continuing City* (1969), *An Exploded View* (1973), *The Echo Gate* (1979) *Gorse Fires* (1991), *The Ghost Orchid* (1995) and *Broken Dishes* (1998).

Lynch, Brian was born in Dublin in 1945. He has published several collections of poetry including *Endsville* (with Paul Durcan, 1967), *Perpetual Star* (1980), *Beds of Down* (1983), *Voices from the Nettleway* (1986) and *Easter Snow – An Island off Ireland* (1992). He is also an art critic, playwright and television dramatist.

McBreen, Joan was born in Sligo in 1946 and lives in Tuam, County Galway. Her poetry is collected in *The Wind Beyond the Wall* (1990), *A Walled Garden in Moylough* (1995) and *Poems Selected and New* (1998).

MacCarthy, Catherine Phil was born in Crecora, County Limerick in 1954. Her poetry collections are *This Hour of the Tide*, (Salmon, 1994) and *The Blue Globe* (Blackstaff 1998). Her work has won several awards and she is currently editor of *Poetry Ireland Review*.

MacDonogh, Steve is a publisher, poet and editor. He is the founder and proprietor of Brandon Book Publishing and the Mount Eagle imprint, based in Dingle, County Kerry.

McGuckian, Medbh was born in Belfast in 1950. Among her most recent books are *Marconi's Cottage* (1991) and *Captain Lavender* (1994). *Selected Poems 1978–1994* appeared in 1997.

Mahon, Derek was born in Belfast in 1941. He has published many collections of poetry, among them *The Hunt By Night* (1982) and *Antarctica* (1985). A *Selected Poems* was published in 1990, *The Hudson Letter* in 1996 and *The Yellow Book* in 1997.

Meehan, Paula was born in Dublin in 1955. She has published five collections of poetry, *Return and No Blame* (1984), *Reading the Sky* 1986), *The Man Who was Marked by Winter* (1991), *Pillow Talk* (1994) and *Mysteries of the Home* (1996).

Monahan, Noel was born in Granard County Longford and now lives in County Cavan. He has won several awards for his poetry and has published two collections: *Opposite Walls* (1991) and *Snowfire* (1995).

Montague, John was born in Brooklyn, NY in 1929 and brought up in County Tyrone He has published more than a dozen collections of poetry, notably *Poisoned Lands* (1961), *The Rough Field* (1972), *A Slow Dance* (1975), *The Great Cloak* (1978) and *The Dead Kingdom* (1988). In 1998 he was named Ireland Professor of Poetry.

Muldoon, Paul was born near Moy in County Armagh in 1955. His published work includes *New Weather* (1973), *Mules* (1977), *Quoof* (1983), *Meeting the British* (1987), and *Madoc: A Mystery* (1990), his latest volume being *New and Selected Poems* (1996).

Murphy, Richard was born in County Galway in 1927. His poetry collections include *Sailing to an Island* (1963), *The Battle of Aughrim* (1968), *High Island* (1974) and *The Price of Stone* (1985).

Ní Chuilleanáin, Eiléan was born in Cork in 1942. She has published seven collections of verse, including *Acts and Monuments* (1972), *Site of Ambush* (1975), *The Magdalene Sermon* (1989) and *Brazen Serpent* (1994).

Ní Dhomhnaill, Nuala was born in Lancashire in 1952 but spent most of her childhood in the Kerry gaeltacht area near Ventry. Her first collection was *An Dealg Droighin* (1991). In collaboration with translators she has published bilingual collections such as *Pharaoh's Daughter* (1990) and *The Astrakhan Cloak* (1992). Her most recent collection is *Spíonáin is Róiseanna*. (1993).

O'Donnell, Mary was born in Monaghan in 1954. She has published three collections of verse, *Reading the Sunflowers in September* (1990), *Spiderwoman's Third Avenue Rhapsody* (1993) and *Unlegendary Heroes* (1998) as well as two novels and a collection of short stories.

O'Donoghue, Bernard was born in County Cork in 1945 and now teaches at Wadham College Oxford. He has published three books of poetry, *Poaching Rights* (1987), *The Weakness* (1991) and *Gunpowder* (1995). His next book, *Here Nor There*, will appear in January 1999.

O'Driscoll, Dennis was born in Thurles, County Tipperary in 1954. His poetry is published in four volumes, *Kist* (1982), *Hidden Extras* (1987), *Long Short Story* (1993) and *Quality Time* (1997).

O'Grady, Desmond was born in Limerick in 1935 and after living abroad for many years returned to settle in Kinsale, County Cork. He has published sixteen collections of poetry, including *The Road Taken, 1956-1996*, nine collections of translated poetry and prose memoirs. He is a member of Aosdána.

O'Hagan, Sheila has published collections including *The Peacock's Eye* and *The Troubled House*. She has won the Patrick Kavanagh and the *Sunday Tribune*-Hennessy awards for poetry.

O'Malley, Mary was born in County Galway. She has published three collections of poetry, *A Consideration of Silk* (1990), *Where the Rocks Float* (1993) and *The Knife in the Wave* (1997).

Ó Searcaigh, Cathal was born in Gortahork in the County Donegal gaeltacht in 1956. His collections include *Miontragéide Cathrach* (1975), *Súile Shuibhne* (1983), *An Bealach 'na Bhaile* (1991) and *Na Buachaillí Bána* (1996).

O'Siadhail, Micheal was born in Dublin in 1947. He has published several collections in Irish; his English-language collections include *Springnight* (1983), *The Chosen Garden* (1990) and *Our Double Time* (1998).

O'Sullivan, Michael was born in Cork City and educated at UCC. He has published three collections of poetry, including *The Physics of Parting* which won the American Cloverdale Prize for poetry in 1993.

Paulin, Tom was born in Leeds in 1949 and reared in Belfast. His published poetry includes *A State of Justice* (1977), *Liberty Tree* (1983), *Fivemiletown* (1987) and *Walking a Line* (1994). He is also a playwright, critic and broadcaster.

Quinn, Justin was born in Dublin in 1968. His first collection of poetry, *The O'o'a'a' Bird* was shortlisted for the 1995 Forward Prize. A second volume, *Privacy*, appeared in 1998.

Scully, Maurice was born in Dublin in 1952. Among his books are *Love Poems and Others* (1981), *Freedoms of Movement* (1987), *The Basic Colours* (1992), *Priority* (1995) and *Steps* (1998).

Sirr, Peter was born in Waterford in 1960. He has published four collections of poetry, *Marginal Zones* (1984), *Talk, Talk* (1987), *Ways of Falling* (1991), and *The Ledger of Fruitful Exchange* (1995). He is co-editor of *Graph: Irish Cultural Review* and Director of the Irish Writers' Centre in Dublin.

Strong, Eithne was born in Glensharrold, County Limerick in 1923. She has published several volumes of poetry, including *Songs of Living* (1961), *Flesh: The Greatest Sin* (1982) and *Spatial Nosing* (1993). She has also published five volumes of Irish poetry, including *Fuil agus Fallaí* (1983) and *Aoife faoi Ghlas* (1990), a collection of short stories and two novels.

Wall, William was born in Whitegate, County Cork in 1955. He has published a volume of poetry, *Mathematics and Other Poems* (1996), short stories and fiction for children.

Wheatley, David was born in Dublin in 1970. *Thirst* (1997), his first poetry collection, won the Rooney Prize in 1998.

Woods, Macdara was born in Dublin in 1942. He is founder/editor of the literary magazine *Cyphers*. He has published several collections of poetry, most recently *Notes from the Countries of Blood-Red Flowers* (1996) and *Selected Poems* (1996). He is a member of Aosdána.